Cross-Cultural Narratives

Stories and Experiences of International Students

Praise for the Book

Through rich and engaging stories, *Cross-Cultural Narratives* offers important personal accounts of the challenges and triumphs of international students navigating diverse and foreign academic and cultural landscapes. This inspiring and thought-provoking collection adds to other noble qualitative documentation of the international student experience.

Anthony L. Pinder
Associate Vice President for Academic Affairs –
Internationalization & Global Engagement
Emerson College, USA

***

This book fills a much-needed gap in the literature on international students by giving them a voice to tell their stories.

Gang Li
Assistant Professor
Trinity Western University, Canada

***

This edited collection of stories offers insight into the concrete details of US life that international students find confounding: that bread is soft and sweet, that everyone asks, "How are you?" but no one wants to know the answer, that fellow students don't know the metric system, and that people are startled if you kiss them on the cheek in greeting. All of these examples, in the students' own voices, will be valuable to practitioners and faculty who want to understand how life on and off campus appears from multiple perspectives.

Martha C. Merrill
Associate Professor, Higher Education
Kent State University, USA

***

I highly recommend this collection to all involved in the field of international education.

Meg Gardinier
Fellow, *STAR Scholars Network, USA*

***

The edited book by Dr. Ammigan is "from international students about international students" and is an excellent contribution! The narratives provide an important glimpse into international students' lived experience and reveal their agency and authorship of their own story

Omolabake (Labake) Fakunle
MSc Education Pathway Coordinator
University of Edinburgh, UK

***

Have you or others at your institution wondered how best to support the international students in your ranks? Dr. Ammigan's book is an ambitious undertaking that chronicles the experiences of international students from a variety of cultural contexts, giving us deeper insights into these students from a first-person perspective.

Emily P. Schell
Developmental and Psychological Sciences
Stanford Graduate School of Education, USA

***

This is a great resource for researchers, university staff, and students to (re)situate themselves in the day-to-day reality of international students at U.S. universities. In our data driven world abounding with echo chambers, it is critical that we as humans continue to nurture and attend to diverse individual narratives of challenge, success, failure, humor, learning, shock, community, belonging, and resiliency. Let us listen to the next generation as they share the ties that bind us across differences.

Nelson Brunsting
Director, RAISE Center
Research Associate Professor, International Studies
Wake Forest University, USA

***

This book makes creative and compelling arguments by exposing lived experiences and stories of international students. By sharing cross-cultural, intercultural, transborder, and/or transnational research strategies, this book, I believe, will reduce pedagogical blind spots, including feelings of alienation, isolation, and outsider, that international students encounter in classrooms and on college campuses.

Marohang Limbu
Associate Professor of Writing, Rhetoric, and American Cultures
Michigan State University, USA

***

This important collection amplifies student voices, offering a wide range of rich experiences. I found myself transported back to my time as an international student, reliving how central it was to my own development, and feeling newly inspired.

Gretchen Rudham
Assistant Professor of Urban Educational Leadership
Morgan State University, USA

Cross-Cultural Narratives
Stories and Experiences of International Students

Living and studying away from home can turn out to be an enriching and rewarding experience for many international students. Yet, many of them struggle to cope with their new university life due to distinct challenges such as cultural differences, language and communication barriers, and a lack of social support. Through a diverse collection of personal essays, this book captures some of the stories of international students as they reflect on their intercultural encounters, expectations, and experiences in their new surroundings and local communities. Essay themes range from culture shock to resilience, and they cover a variety of topics including the ways students change and gain new perspectives by being away from their comfort zone, the feeling of isolation and being an outsider, and the uncertainties of making new friends.

This book provides readers with a unique opportunity to *walk a mile in the shoes* of an international student. It also highlights the importance of a strong support system for students in both the curricular and co-curricular settings and offers insights to international educators and university administrators into creating a welcoming environment that fosters international understanding and cross-cultural awareness on campus.

Editor

Ravichandran Ammigan, PhD, is Associate Deputy Provost for International Programs and Assistant Professor of Education at the University of Delaware.

Cross-Cultural Narratives
Stories and Experiences of International Students

Edited by

Ravichandran Ammigan
University of Delaware, USA

OJED
JOURNAL OF
INTERNATIONAL
STUDENTS
STAR SCHOLARS

★STARSCHOLARS
N E T W O R K

First Published 2021

by

STAR Scholars

In collaboration with

Open Journals in Education

Journal of International Students

and

University of Delaware

Category

Education/International Students

Series

Comparative and International Education

Typeset in Garamond

Series Editor
Krishna Bista

Project Advisor
Chris R. Glass

Copy Editor
Sanoya Amienyi
Osa Amienyi

Cover Design
Srdjan Marjanovic

Printed in the United States of America

Editor
Ravichandran Ammigan

ISBN: 978-1-7364699-0-3

© STAR Scholars

Library of Congress Control Number:
2021900779

Cross-Cultural Narratives: Stories and
Experiences of International Students

Subject: Education/International Students –
United States | International Education |
Student Mobility | Comparative Education

Names: Ravichandran Ammigan (editor),
Krishna Bista (series editor)

Library of Congress
US Programs, Law, and Literature Division
Cataloging in Publication Program
101 Independence Avenue, S.E.
Washington, DC 20540-4283

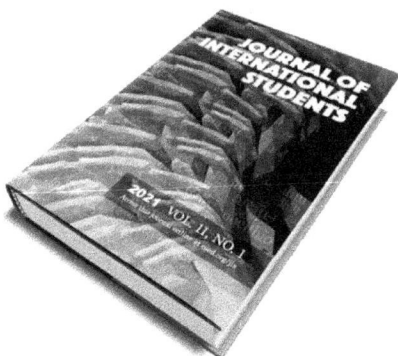

OJED

OPEN JOURNALS IN EDUCATION

Open Journals in Education (OJED) publishes high quality peer reviewed, open access journals based at research universities. OJED uses the Open Journal System platform, where readers can browse by subject, drill down to journal level to find the aims, scope, and editorial board for each individual title, as well as search back issues. None of the OJED journals charge fees to individual authors thanks to the generous support of our institutional sponsors. OJED journals benefit from the editorial, production, and marketing expertise of our team of volunteers.

Explore our journals at www.ojed.org

Higher Education Politics & Economics

Journal of Comparative and International Higher Education

Journal of Underrepresented & Minority Progress

Journal of Human Services

Journal of Interdisciplinary Studies in Education

Journal of Development Education

Journal of Trauma Studies in Education

Journal of School Administration Research and Development

Journal of Global Literacies, Technologies & Emerging Pedagogies

International Journal of Multidisciplinary Perspectives in Higher Education

Contents

About the Editor

Ravichandran Ammigan, PhD, is Associate Deputy Provost for International Programs and Assistant Professor of Education at the University of Delaware. With over 20 years of experience in the field of international higher education, he has served in a number of leadership and administrative positions in international student and scholar services, education abroad, and admissions and recruitment. Dr. Ammigan's research focuses on the international student experience at institutions of higher education globally, with a particular emphasis on student satisfaction and support services. Originally from the island of Mauritius, he first came to the United States as an international student himself and stayed to work as an expatriate. He holds a BA in Business Administration, an MA in Communication, and a PhD in Higher Education Internationalization.

Some of his recent publications include:
- Ammigan, R., Dennis, J. L., & Jones, E. (2021). The differential impact of learning experiences on international student satisfaction and institutional recommendation. *Journal of International Students*, *11*(2).
- Ammigan, R. (2019). Institutional satisfaction and recommendation: What really matter to international students? *Journal of International Students*, 9(1), 253–272.
- Ammigan, R., & Jones, E. (2018). Improving the student experience: Learning from a comparative study of international student satisfaction. *Journal of Studies in International Education*, 22(4), 283-301.

Preface

The presence of international students at institutions of higher education represents a tremendous opportunity for fostering international understanding and cross-cultural awareness among students, faculty, staff, and local community members. Decades-old literature provides evidence that international students can be an invaluable resource in developing holistic global engagement and intercultural competence across academic and non-academic settings. This diverse community of students makes important intellectual, cultural, and economic contributions to their host university and country, and can serve as a key aspect in advancing internationalization, inclusivity, and diversity efforts on campus. For these benefits to be realized, however, institutions must remain aware of the differential needs and expectations of their students.

There are many challenges that international students often face as they adjust to their new university life overseas. These usually include language barriers, acculturative stress, educational difficulties, and a lack of social support. As such, it is imperative that institutions actively assess their students' experiences and develop interventions, resources, and services that support their educational goals and academic success. Reflective essays can be a useful tool in providing qualitative feedback and insight to international educators and administrators. This book, *Cross-Cultural Narratives: Stories and Experiences of International Students*, showcases a selection of personal stories from hundreds of essays that highly talented international students wrote over the years, as part of an annual essay contest hosted by the University of Delaware's Center for Global Programs and Services.

The assembled essays in this book capture some powerful narratives from a variety of students across different nationalities, levels of study, and academic disciplines. Topics range from cultural misunderstandings and adaptation to local traditions, to defining moments at the airport, in local grocery stores and restaurants, and during Thanksgiving dinner. Others wrote about their own self, personal growth and development, their transformational experience of living and studying in the US, and their participation in thought-provoking classes, internships, and community activities, despite the initial struggles of isolation, difficulty in making friends, and lack of confidence in communicating in a second language.

I, for one, can relate to these anecdotes as a former international student in the United States over 20 years ago, scrambling to navigate a new environment, a new culture, and new protocols for the first time. Yet, I vividly remember my

Resident Assistant who asked me how I was doing and actually stopped to listen to my story; how my English professor found time after class to assist me with an internship application; and when my soccer teammates went out of their way to plan a birthday get-together for me. Those were all impactful moments that really mattered and helped me persevere as a student, far from family and old friends. I now have the privilege and profoundly validating responsibility, as an international educator and administrator at my institution, to sustain a collaborative service model that supports the acculturation, well-being, and success of our international student community.

The purpose of the international student essay contest is to give students another avenue to share their experiences and voice their concerns, and at the same time create an opportunity for local community members to "walk a mile in their shoes," with the goal of maintaining a welcoming and globally friendly climate on campus. Our hope is that these poignant stories, although not to be generalized, will reach a wider audience and serve as a point of reference for understanding and contextualizing the diversity of perspectives from international students, bearing in mind that support services for this community must be intentional, strategic, and adaptable.

Ravichandran Ammigan, PhD

Acknowledgements

I am truly grateful to all the University of Delaware students who participated in the essay contest beginning the fall of 2013, and to the staff and faculty who encouraged them to write and share their stories.

I would like to express my sincere thanks to the UD Division of Student Life, the Graduate College, and the Office of the Provost for their continued partnership and sponsorship of the international student essay contest. Heartfelt thanks go to all the judges who have served on the selection committee over the years, and to the staff of the Center for Global Programs and Services for their tireless commitment and dedication to international education.

I wish to convey my deepest appreciation to Dr. Krishna Bista (Founding Editor of Journal of International Students), Dr. Chris Glass (Editor-in-Chief), and colleagues at the STAR Scholars Network and at the Open Journals in Education, a consortium of the professional journals, for their assistance and coordination in publishing this book. Without their support and guidance, this book would not have become a reality.

I would like to thank the following colleagues for their feedback on the early draft of this book as well as for their endorsements:

- Anthony L. Pinder, *Emerson College, USA*
- Gang Li, *Trinity Western University, Canada*
- Martha C. Merrill, *Kent State University, USA.*
- Meg Gardinier, *STAR Scholars Network, USA*
- Emily P. Schell, *Stanford Graduate School of Education, USA*
- Nelson Brunsting, *Wake Forest University, USA*
- Marohang Limbu, *Michigan State University, USA*
- Gretchen Rudham, *Morgan State University, USA*
- Omolabake (Labake) Fakunle, *University of Edinburgh, UK*

Ravichandran Ammigan

1

America – A Whole New World!

Sarah Yacoba Coomson, Ghana

I am Ghanaian, and I have lived in Ghana, West Africa most of my life. Often times when people hear of Africa, they immediately think of a desolate third world place, with unexposed and somewhat backward humans struggling to get the very basic of life's requirements. Truth is, this couldn't be further from the reality of Africa today. Africa has and continues to morph into a well-developed and contemporary region amidst actual struggles and I believe with time the world will be open to the true state of Africa. That notwithstanding, coming to UD and America has opened a whole new world to me for which experiences I cannot even begin to recount.

Prior to my coming here, I had spent some considerable time in the United Kingdom and also some countries in Europe. I had also previously visited the United States once and these collective experiences made me confident that my transition into the American lifestyle would be breezy. That said however, nothing could minimize the excitement at the idea that America would be my primary home for the next couple of years, and this excitement has not diminished yet. This new reality and excitement became even more authentic when I walked into my rented apartment. I remember darting a quick glance around and then turning to my husband in nervous excitement as we smiled to each other, our minds seemingly communicating telepathically. In no time, we agreed to head out to the supermarket to get a few essentials, which was where I got my first reality check in this new land – I needed a car! Now having a car has always been somewhat of a normal thing in Ghana, but not necessarily a necessity because of the abundance of public transport continuously plying the roads. The transport system in London too was so efficient that having a car was tossed to the back burner but here I was just realizing that this machine which I had never considered would be vital in making my stay here comfortable, and for a seamless fusion into an American lifestyle.

Now when I settled into the business of why I am actually here, another reality dawned on me. I remember the first day I stepped into my lab at the University of Delaware, and the feeling of immense fulfillment as I smiled at the organization and the quality of equipment ready for my use. The friendliness and willingness to help totally demystified graduate education for me. The pressure I had built up in my mind stemming from possible pitfalls in my knowledge repertoire quickly dissipated as I realized that ready and friendly help was available. Unlike the professors and instructors in Ghana who often come across as unapproachable demi-gods, I am particularly pleased that my supervisor takes special interest in my progress, is willing to have discussions and readily responds to emails, some of which I must admit I am even too hesitant to send. The relief and excitement every time my email beeps with a response almost immediately still gives me the fuzzies to this day.

I got another cultural shock as I took a couple of undergraduate students through some courses. Now I understand for Americans it is generally typical to express one's self freely, however in Ghana it is strictly forbidden to talk back to anyone in any superior position regardless of how right you may think you are. Conversely, the brazen nature of these young Americans as they express opposing views and indeed themselves, their ability to engage in very hearty discussions and probe novel concepts will remain with me wherever I go, and even as I continue to peel back the layers of "Africanness" to seamlessly fuse into the American system at the same time being conscious to not abandon totally the values and cultures that make me African.

As I continue on this adventure, I realize more and more that there is no place like America. The highways are expansive, the supermarkets grand and the system all around efficient. Boy! This land of the free with individuals from literally every corner of the world chasing opportunities in trying to be better. I have so far travelled to New York and Florida states and the differences between them is testament to the uniqueness of America. My taste buds have been excited by cuisines from different parts of the world. The COVID pandemic highlighted the efficiency of the address and delivery systems, which may be taken for granted but based off of where I am coming from is quite commendable. I now understand why America holds such global appeal and I could not be happier to call it my home for the next few years. I know and look forward to more culturally diverse experiences to make me a more rounded global person.

First Steps of a Blue Hen

Abhinav Prabhakar, India

My journey at the University of Delaware and in the US began a few months before the pandemic struck. While I was still getting exposed to a different social and professional environment, the coronavirus situation brought about unforeseen challenges and altered things significantly. It called for greater adaptability and resilience when I had just begun to embrace and feel at ease with an unfamiliar culture. In the process, however, I discovered unique learning opportunities, each imparting valuable life lessons. Here, I chronicle my experiences as an international student in the US prior to and during the pandemic.

Life before the pandemic was packed with excitement as I prepared to embark on a new phase of my career in the 'land of opportunities' albeit a very distant land. I was in high spirits in anticipation of new experiences and greater learning opportunities. However, I could not help feeling a bit anxious about my survival skills so far away from home and in a different cultural environment. I had just attained the status of an uncle, with the birth of my niece, and the thought of leaving her and the rest of my family added to my uneasiness. Moreover, as someone who values cultural identity, I was unsure if my cultural background would be understood or respected in a foreign land. Despite these concerns, I undertook the 28-hour journey from India filled with hope, promise and plenty of family support.

During my first few days in the US, I befriended an extremely warm and welcoming family couple. Having two sons who pursued graduate studies away from home, they were all too familiar with the needs of a new student. They offered to become my host family and helped me settle down into my daily routine. In most of my public interactions, I tread cautiously because I was unsure about local conversational customs and I tried my best not to create awkward situations. As I began to expand my social circle, a frequent question I got was 'What part of India are you from?' Rather than mention my town, city or state I would simply say, 'From the south', but I was pleasantly surprised when some people knew the names of prominent southern Indian cities.

One of my early challenges was adapting to drinking water from the faucet. On asking my apartment owner about facilities for drinking water, he said "You can get it from the taps." I was shocked as tap water is unfit for drinking back home and I foolishly asked, "Are you sure this is safe?" It took a great deal of persuasion on his part to convince me about its safety and hygiene. I took a few nervy gulps from a glass of tap water; I survived but decided to purchase a water purifier to feel reassured. Grocery shopping in US supermarkets was another initially uncomfortable task. In my hometown, shopping is largely ad-hoc with quick, regular visits to roadside markets and small stores, but the sheer size of supermarkets here with several aisles of grocery items meant shopping took much longer. Frequent trips were inconvenient, and I had to adopt bulk buying practices. Moreover, it took a while for me to realize that when the cashier or store assistant says, 'Have a good one', it refers to 'Have a nice day' and not 'Enjoy your purchase.' As time went by, I became more confident and capable in communicating with others.

I was gradually beginning to feel comfortable in my new environment, then the pandemic hit. The resulting lockdown meant two things: a new learning and working style, and limited social and outdoor activities. Initially, I thought all this would not last very long and we would be back to normal within a couple of months. But the pandemic had other ideas, forcing the year to be played out indoors and online. The biggest impact for me was rescheduling my work-related goals and putting on hold travel plans of visiting my family. I had to extend my timelines because on-campus work in laboratories and offices was suspended. This resulted in great uncertainty and quite a bit of frustration. I also missed spending time in the library and student centers or catching up with friends over coffee.

As the year wound down, it was time to welcome the Thanksgiving season but in a very different way amid the pandemic. Coming from a culture where traditional and religious festivals are celebrated with much enthusiasm, it was disappointing not to experience a local tradition fully and freely. After all, my purpose here was not purely academic but to learn about culture too. My host family organized a Thanksgiving lunch for a small gathering to which I was very kindly invited. They took the trouble of ensuring physical distancing and providing sanitizing facilities. It was an educational afternoon for me where I learned about the significance of the tradition and got to experience a little of American family life. I was thankful for the opportunity to be part of a family at a time I felt I needed it most. I tried to take advantage of the virtual reality whenever I could. For instance, seminars and lectures were held online and recorded so I could watch them in my spare time. Moreover, I had opportunities to participate in several online discussion forums that boosted my self-confidence and skills in oral communication. The year 2020 was a difficult year to navigate but I am fortunate to have made it through with patience and perseverance. More importantly, I learned to be grateful and appreciate all that I have especially when others elsewhere were struggling in worse ways. I head into 2021 with the same belief that brought me here, of hope and promise of better times.

3

Making a Home Away from Home, Outside the Comfort Zone

Emma Perichon, France

In the blink of an eye, here I am, on the verge of graduating from the University of Delaware. Four years had just flown by. But still, I am not ready to move on from these simultaneously wonderful, confusing, rewarding and irreplaceable years that have made me the person that I am today. When I close my eyes, I retrace my first time walking around campus and picturing myself as a student, imagining what it would feel like to be lounging in the quad, or rushing to make it to class on time. Today, I feel connected to the places I pass each day as they are infused with memories: jumping in the South green fountain, picnics on the green, marathon study sessions and tears shed in the Morris library.

As an international student, I was looking for a fresh experience. I wanted to abandon my comfort zone and immerse myself in a different culture. That breathless leap of faith is at once exciting and oh-so-terrifying, a butterfly made of lead roiling my stomach on the day I landed in my freshman dorm. I felt unsure whether I would 'fit in' with others and anxious about what would come next. The first night, I made a promise to myself: I would not permit uncertainty to obstruct opportunity. After all, the hard part was over. I had already made that first and biggest step moving abroad to study. I had arrived, and while I did not know what would happen next, I knew one thing was certain. Now was not the time to chicken out.

Leaving your comfort zone means taking steps that may in other circumstances leave you paralyzed with fear. And it is not the big things like navigating visas or flying halfway across the world. No, true growth lies in the small victories of everyday life. The courage to introduce myself to the girl sitting next to me in class, who led me to meeting a true friend in my major, a study partner who will be standing next to me during our graduation ceremony. Finding my voice to say "Hi" leads to shared memories and a friendship that I will carry long after I throw my cap in the air.

Studying abroad can still feel scary and leave you feeling like a fish out of water. I often felt apprehensive that my own culture, my experiences, and my humor were out of place and that people would not get it, that they would judge me and find me strange. For my part, I find many things in this place, this culture, and this language hard to wrap my head around, too. Sometimes the way I would say things would sound a little funny and make people laugh. To be fair, hippopotamus is NOT an easy word to pronounce! But what I love about UD is that here, the differences make you unique, they create laughter, start new conversations, and ultimately bring people closer together.

Now firmly out of my comfort zone, my second step was to leverage the many resources available to students. By attending events like the club fair, I was able to pursue topics and pastimes that sparked my interest and explore them, wear them for a day to see how they fit. I learned how a television studio worked, how to put a show together and write a script from scratch. Those skills were not only fascinating but helpful for my writing skills and a deeper understanding of how to communicate with others. In another club, I traveled to Chicago and learned about the merits of promoting EQ in the workplace at a student conference. I met high-flying CEOs and made connections across my chosen industry.

The best decision I made far and away from my comfort zone was joining the University's Greek life. At first, all I had ever known about fraternities and sororities were boiled down stereotypes and cliches from the movies. However, I was impressed with the size of the Greek community when I first toured the University of Delaware and caught myself wondering what it would feel like to belong to such a large and diverse community. This was a surefire way to meet lots of new people with whom I shared similar interests and values. This motivated me to 'rush' for a sorority and see if they would accept me. Once again, the dizzying feelings of fear and excitement pushed me over a new edge of comfort and delivered me to an even greater experience in University life.

With my comfort zone a distant memory, I met girls from all different backgrounds filled with contagious positive energy. This has led to truly unforgettable memories, finding in myself the capacity to lead and organize, and forging deep roots to my closest friends. Our adventures took us on trips to Europe and across the US to learn about each other's experiences, in which we discovered that all of us arrived at University excited and terrified, that we all really left behind a comfort zone to try new things and meet new people. We all shared many of the same feelings and desires before ultimately finding each other. This journey to seek out what is different and to try out the new ultimately led me to finding people that I trust and learn from the unfamiliar. This fulfilled that itch that led me to study abroad.

This community has become my home, an expansion of my comfort zone. With the support of my friends, my classmates, my professors, and alumni, I can count on this shared home to carry me onto the next adventure, the next launch and that new edge. Only this time, I'll have close friends and great memories to accompany those feelings of excitement and fear.

4

Home Away from Home

Jady Young Perez, Panama

"Mom, I got into UD!" I still remember how excited I was to be the first one in my family to have the opportunity to study outside of my home country, Panama, and also be the first one to pursue a degree in Engineering. I was so excited that I did a countdown every single day leading up to move-in day at the University of Delaware. I kept practicing my English with people around me including my mom, which really irritated her considering she does not speak English and would constantly watch YouTube videos titled "A Day in The Life of a College Student." Once I moved in, I remember walking up to the green, and feeling a sense of fulfillment. I felt invincible. However, as a couple of weeks went by, it became very difficult to be far from my family, friends, food, and more while at the same time navigating a different country, culture, and a rigorous curriculum.

I knew that an Engineering curriculum was going to be hard, but I had no idea how much harder it was going to be along with living in a new country and being a minority. On my very first midterm in college, which was for Calculus I, I got a 58%. For context, I had never gotten a bad grade in school – I graduated as salutatorian of my class. I was devastated.

The worst part was, I saw my grade while eating at the Caesar Rodney cafeteria, and without even noticing tears were rolling down my face. It was humiliating. I kept thinking "how can I be a successful engineer if I can't even pass a calculus exam?", "maybe I should leave, I don't know if I can do this..." On top of that, I was struggling to make friends, which is something that I had never struggled with, so I felt like a complete loser. I felt that it was hard to connect with others because my day-to-day experiences and likings in music, food, etc. were so different than the typical American. I even had an awkward interaction while I was being introduced to someone because I leaned in for a kiss on the cheek (which is normal in my country, and I had, of course, forgotten that it wasn't here) and she seemed so uncomfortable that she just walked away. I kept thinking that maybe I wasn't ready to be in another country, and that I should just give up. But then I remembered that I was not getting this degree just for me, but to make my family proud and all the Latina women in STEM out there. I knew I was capable and that I just had to keep pushing.

I decided to come up with a plan to improve my grades and social life. I got a planner and started to plan my days to the minute to make sure I was using my time wisely. I planned not only when I was going to do my homework and at what times, but also when I was going to eat, have leisure time, etc. I also planned weekly goals on how to make more friends, which included bullet points such as "you will talk to someone at the dining hall, and you will not be scared!" and "talk to people in class – ask for their snapchat (I think this is the social media platform Americans prefer to use?)" Looking back, it was definitely a little out there (and embarrassing) to plan my days like this, but it paid off. I became more social, and surely enough, I started to get to know others and make friends quickly. I was able to pick up on slang and what clothes girls preferred to wear, which made it easier to interact with others without looking like an outsider. Also, during an international coffee hour organized by the International Student Office, I was able to meet a group of students from Latin America that are still my friends three years later, which was very helpful because they basically became my support group.

I also made it my goal to teach others about my country. Panama is a very small, yet beautiful country full of diversity and beautiful beaches. I knew I wanted to make sure that I planted a seed in everyone's head about Panama's existence and its beauty. Once I had enough trust with friends, I will tell them about all of my favorite experiences in my country, and typical cultural differences between Panama and the US so they could have a better understanding of my experience as an international student. It was exciting to see them eager to learn more about my country. It truly felt like an honor to represent my country and share it with others at UD.

Fast-forward three years and I am now a senior. I have passed every single one of my classes and maintained a good GPA. I have had two internships, have been able to make meaningful connections with both my professors and friends, and have truly enjoyed being at UD, all while being in a pandemic for the last year. I can finally say that UD feels like home. I had to give up a lot, but I was also able to gain so much from it. I am now more confident, strong, smart, and I know that my future will be bright thanks to UD. My freshman year-self is extremely proud of how far I have come, and I am sure this is only the beginning of the many more goals I will accomplish. I am saddened that my journey at UD will be over this year, but I know I plan on coming back for events such as Alumni Weekend, and to visit restaurants such as Roots, Ali Baba, and El Diablo on Main Street, obviously! I now look forward to not only representing my country, but also UD. I will forever be a Blue Hen in my heart.

5

From Dreaming to Doing

Norah Almousa, Saudi Arabia

When I was a student at college, my friend told me about her sister who was studying in the US and I started to dream of studying there also to pursue advanced degrees. I stayed true to my dream and did whatever I could to achieve it. I kept this dream in front of my eyes, so I graduated with high grades. I was picked from more than 20,000 students to get a scholarship to study in the US. Now I feel that I put my feet on the first step to achieve my goal.

It was not easy to make this decision to travel abroad for the first time in my life. I prepared and dreamed about this day with happiness and excitement to see the world and learn new things. However, not everything happens as we want it to be. There are obstacles that will appear, but we need to overcome them. In my country, I used to be surrounded by my family and get help and support from them, but when I arrived at the Washington airport, I asked myself what I needed to do to get to Delaware. I realized that I was alone now, and I needed to make all these decisions by myself. At first, I could not do everything by myself. I called my mother every day to ask her what I should do about even simple things such as making food and going to different places. However, day after day I noticed that I was becoming a stronger and more independent woman who could stand on her own feet without needing help. These situations have shaped me and made me a more responsible person.

Struggling with English before I came to the US, I only had the basic language proficiency to communicate with others. However, once I arrived here, I realized that the English language was completely different from what I thought it was. One day, an American friend invited me to a party, but I could not fit in with them. I felt frustrated because I had studied hard to improve my English, but I still faced difficulty to communicate. Sometimes I ask myself if I am in the right place or not and if I can do it. However, I was lucky that I was surrounded by a good host family, teachers, tutors, and friends who always supported me and encouraged me to persevere. In addition, I changed my idea about how difficult English was, and suddenly everything was much easier for me. I learned how important it is to be more positive and how that would affect my life. In conclusion, learning English at the UD English Language Institute (ELI) has taught me a lot of things, not just English but also about life. I have expanded my knowledge about other topics that have opened my eyes about my life.

Shutting down school and switching from in-person classes to online classes was not easy, especially for learners of languages. Learning behind these screens has been difficult. When we communicate with each other, we sometimes have difficulty understanding each other and that is what makes the process so hard.

Avoiding distractions such as the phone in order to focus on my lessons is also not easy. At the ELI, there are teachers who come up with creative ways to deal with these issues and make the classes fun and enjoyable. Furthermore, with online learning, I have built a strong relationship with my tutors that would never have happened if there had been no online classes. I spend two to three hours a day with them, and I learn many things that I could not have learned from just studying or traveling.

Last year was different for me not just because I live in the US, but also because of the pandemic that impacted the whole world. When the pandemic started, I decided to go back to my country. I thought it would be safer for me if I were with my family and in my country.

But because of the travel risks and safety issues, I changed my mind and canceled all my plans and stayed here at UD. During that time, I was very concerned and wondered whether I would ever see my family again. After I shared my feelings and fears about COVID-19 with my teacher, she gave me advice that I believe changed my life forever. I started to look for new activities that I could do during this time, such as meditation and yoga, which have become a part of my life. Finally, I realize that the global pandemic has reminded us to be grateful for what we have and not take any of it for granted.

In conclusion, I think that this is one of the best decisions that I have ever made because living in the US and studying at UD and the ELI have transformed and changed me a lot. These enormous changes will shape me in a great way. The ELI has given me so much, and I am happy and excited to say that I will be a member of UD next fall semester.

6

The Moment I Lost My Voice

Essa Nahari, Saudi Arabia

Have you ever loved someone from their voice alone without ever seeing their face? This is how relationships for millions of people in the Gulf of Arab states work.

For a while I kept wondering why my best friend's girlfriend believed in his love even though he had never seen her face, since the Niqab kept her face hidden. "Along with her magical eyes, what really attracted me was her musical voice," he said. Then after four months of conversations, he finally saw his girlfriend's face for the first time, but still her voice stuck in his mind more than anything else!

When my friend had to travel to the United States for his master's degree, they assured each other they would stay together. However, the time zone was a stumbling block to stay in touch because his sleep time overlapped with her breaks from her university where she could call him away from her strict family. She would send him occasional texts of photos of herself, but she could not call. Although he still could see her face, something was missing. Her voice had disappeared, and a love story died.

The bitterness of my friend's story made me eager to explore the secrets of sounds observing that readers need to associate with tone as much as with words. As a reader whose life was flooded with books and reading reviews, I learned that books, including fiction and non-fiction, could not be scientifically analyzed, but they have to be felt by sympathizing with the depths of the author's heart. I accordingly acknowledged that each writer has a distinctly personal tone and orientation. For example, if lovers of philosophical novels were given an unknown piece from *Life is Elsewhere* (Milan Kundera), they would easily recognize the author from the evocative writing rhythm.

Recognizing that sound plays an essential role in reflecting culture, dignity, and love, I thought, "What if I lost the voice that represents my thoughts?" That is exactly what happened in 2016 when I wrote a passage on Multiculturalism. After a competition with 14,000 readers, I reached the list of 40 qualified to be among the ten speakers to deliver their speeches on a major stage. During the first rehearsals, I was terrified and put the microphone aside, sneaking from the stage while tears raced down my cheeks. I lost hope and thought only about my parents and three beautiful sisters who waited for me on the other side of the country, 1,400 kilometers away.

Then, gathering my courage, I forced myself back to the stage again. Crying in front of my competitors brought me to realize the real challenge is not to defeat others but understand and master the self until the best comes out. Fate gave me another opportunity to speak about my experience in reading in "I-inspire Talks" in front of 4,000 people. At the end of the event, I was astonished to see a woman turning toward me with tears staining her Niqab.

The tears signified the reflection of my words on her love for reading and writing—she was young and wished she would have more opportunities to achieve her dreams.

During my press work, I have become acquainted with the meaning of not being heard every time a report of mine is not published because it conflicts with the newspaper's policy or style. However, I discovered that my voice will remain audible as long as it is dedicated to speaking to people's hearts. The real achievement is not in greatness of the theater on which I stand, or the importance of the newspaper I write in, rather in hearts which have been inspired: whether in a café, bar, or even a nook where one of the homeless reads a book while a boy beside him begs his father to buy it.

My First American Football Game!

Carolina Gomez, Colombia

"So, if the player can run all the way to the opponent's end zone and put the ball down, he scores a touchdown for six points - you understand?" I still looked puzzled. All I knew was the fact that the University of Delaware (UD) was winning, and I was just happy to be there. The energy and atmosphere that filled the stadium were electric and could energize anyone, much like the "soccer" games back home in Colombia. My first experience watching American football was an interesting, yet very confusing one, overall. As I stood there and cheered our team on, it suddenly hit me - my experience at UD when I first arrived wasn't that different. At times I felt like I was home, while in other moments, I felt entirely like an alien.

While I was back in my home country, I was excited to finally attend college and begin a new adventure, or rather a new chapter in my life. However, as my mother finally got ready to leave and I was settled into my room, I realized I was just as scared as I was excited. Even if I wanted to, I could not dwell on it for too long. Sure enough, I heard footsteps approaching the room. The door opened. I finally got to meet my American roommate along with her family. I got up, introduced myself, and greeted them the only way I knew how; a tight hug followed by a brief kiss on the cheek. My roommate and her family were taken aback by an unusual greeting they'd never seen. Five minutes into my university experience, I had already noticed a key difference between home and here - greetings. Much to my relief, my roommate's family must have quickly realized this difference and hugged me back just like someone would at home. I must admit it felt good to be able to show someone my culture and for them to understand it too, even for such a small thing. As my UD experience progressed, I noticed more of these differences. Some were larger and more noticeable than others.

One of the largest differences was the food. The first things that I started to crave were my empanadas, sweet plantain and *sancocho* (a chicken soup that is eaten with banana), which were completely different from the food served at the dining hall. This was extremely difficult for me since the food that I've grown up with all my life was suddenly nowhere to be seen. I took to American food cautiously and with the help of my friends, I learnt to appreciate it more and more. One dessert I grew to love especially was ice cream, the one I tried for the first time at the football game at the UDairy Creamery. Much to my surprise, I learnt to take this change in a new perspective over time. I tried new foods from other cultures, all the while learning to appreciate home food even more. I took comfort in watching the experienced Latino community that found its way to make the most of their mundane American lives, while celebrating their own culture, food and roots. I watched them and continued to slowly pick up on how my life wouldn't just be easier, but also a whole new enjoyable experience living here.

Another small difference was the fact the United States does not use the metric system like most of the outside world. I never gave it any thought until my first Biology lab. All the students were required to put down their heights in centimeters on the whiteboard. As the class struggled to pull out their phones and attempt to convert their heights to the metric system, I instantly walked up to the board to write my height down. I was met with curious and inquisitive looks as to why someone would know that in the first place.

Situations like these allowed me to have interesting and stereotype-breaking conversations with my fellow students. As I found myself answering these questions more, I realized that my culture and identity was just as important to others around me as it was to myself, and that the students here truly cared about it and respected it. Even if they found it hilarious at times, I was never truly embarrassed because the laughter was always followed up with intellectual and inquisitive questions to know more about me and why I do things the way I do. Instead of being met with "that's weird", I heard a lot more of "that's really cool I want to visit Colombia now!!". And these conversations went both ways. Just as they learnt a lot about me and where I came from, I got to learn a lot about America and broke a lot of my own personal stereotypes that I had developed from Hollywood and other media outlets. The United States wasn't all glamorous with its flashy cars and beautiful beaches, there was so much more to it that UD has managed to show me through its wonderful campus and people. The colorful trees that turned campus into a vibrant rainbow during fall, the smiling faces that greeted me as I walked around, the hardworking and honest people who work to make this place feel so much like home and a successful place of learning.

I was once a student who felt both at home and completely out of place in the sea of yellow and blue fans at a football game. But with time, I've come to realize that every single individual in that stadium was probably just as different and unique as me, and that is what makes UD so special. I've come to know that we can overcome differences, teach one another new experiences and cultures, and help each other realize our dreams and education while enjoying every second of it. This is what my American experience has been like.

8

From Lima to Newark: Cultural Impressions

Josefina Fernandez-Davila, Peru

Two years ago, I embarked on my journey from the capital of Lima to "The First State" of Delaware, away from my family, my friends, and all that I found familiar. It was a scary thought, leaving everything behind to start over. However, I was determined to step out of the little social bubble I had been living in for eighteen years, with an open heart and mind. I had been to the US before starting college, so I was well aware of the several traditions Americans generally embrace, but I was an outsider. I watched their portrayal in movies, casually rubbed against it on the streets during my travels and glanced at it in golf tournaments. While I did this, I was still under the protective cloak of my own culture and family, but it was quickly stripped off as I stepped on campus for the first time, knowing this would be my home, my new reality, for the following four years. Holidays like Thanksgiving, Saint Patrick's Day and Fourth of July were insignificant to me, since I had no clue what they really meant to those who celebrated them. The idea of living with two roommates at eighteen seemed peculiar to my relatives and friends. I had no clue that, after two years on campus, I would become part of my own family of sisters and brothers that, I am sure, will last a lifetime.

In Peru, you operate in different spheres that rarely communicate with one another. There is a designated time and place for study, for family and for friends. Here, the lines pertaining to work and friendships are blurred. I will go study with my colleagues and grab lunch with my peers before class on a daily basis. My two roommates, who are also my teammates, are my family away from home. They will always be there for me. I have merged my bubbles into one. However, the aspects and thought processes my culture raised me in remain embedded in my brain.

There are some cultural aspects that differ between Peru and the US. For instance, in Peru, it is completely normal for a young adult to live with their parents while going to college and continue to do so until they get married or are financially stable to move out on their own. I have found that in the States this is sometimes frowned upon. Teenagers and young adults are usually encouraged by their parents to be independent, move out of the house and get a job as soon as they get out of college. I have noticed that most even move out of their home state to pursue career opportunities and further develop themselves at a professional level. That is what I found the most appealing of all. Back home, I would never have considered moving out of my parents' home. Although the idea still seems foreign to me, I have slowly been starting to understand their value to others.

Generally, the Hispanic culture has a very distinct approach when it comes to family. In one sense, everyone is family. Our greetings are physical and way of talking flamboyant compared to the way it is done in America. I clearly remember move in day, when I was a freshman on campus. I was extremely excited and nervous about meeting new people and making new friends. Since I had never shared a room with anyone before, the thought of having two roommates was daunting. Will I like them? Will they like me back? Are we going to get along? What if they snore really loudly? I was full of questions. After I was done dropping my belongings in the tiny move-in cart, one of my older teammates helped me climb up to George Read's third floor, room 312, ready to meet my new fellow hens.

As soon as I opened the door, I saw my new roommate, a fellow student athlete freshman from the field hockey team. She came up to me with a confident stride and huge smile on her face, stretching her open hand towards mine. However, I didn't shake her hand back. I went for the standard, habitual Peruvian greeting, a big hug and a kiss on the cheek. Sarah was completely taken aback. She had never been greeted in such a way, specifically by a complete stranger. I was quick to realize my mistake and took immediate action to explain myself. I quickly pointed out that kissing and hugging strangers is a normal act in Hispanic countries. She laughed it off and we kept talking about all the differences our cultures had and how unique they were from one another. On that day, thanks to Sarah, I learned that Americans value and respect each other's personal space. Greetings are formal and small talk is expected. Slowly, I learned how to accommodate myself into the status quo, while I made sure to give the occasional kiss and hug when I greeted a fellow peer. Fitting in does not mean changing one's habits to accommodate those of others; it means to teach others your ways, and to learn from them, so we can all be accepting and understanding of different cultures.

I always thought that my life in the States would be utterly different from my life back in Peru. Nevertheless, to my surprise, I have found the pleasures of friends that turned into family, a passion for golf that became my job, and a chance to receive an exceptional education on the land of opportunity and freedom. What I am most grateful for is the encouragement I had from my peers to embrace and be proud of my culture. I am proud to say that I am a Latina woman studying in Delaware. And I am proud of this cultural journey I have embarked on. I am excited to see what this amazing institution has in store for me for the next two years.

9

Bread in Deutschland

Fabian Martin Rempfer, Germany

When I decided to study in the US, I thought that it would be an easy transition for me coming from Germany. With this creative piece, I want to share my story about how the differences were more shocking than expected but I learned to deal with them and adapted to my surroundings, coming to like and enjoy the differences.

I am a twenty-seven-year-old man who has been able to fend for himself since the age of twelve, and I thought I had figured out America. Five years of American literature had convinced me that I knew everything needed, that I would adapt right away to a novel culture. I thought it would be easy considering that I am from Germany and believed my world to be similar.

But, on my second day in the US, an advisor took us on a shopping trip to Walmart. Upon entering the immense building, I was immediately disabused; I felt like an ant amongst giants. I wandered just to find myself again in the garden section, or tire section, or *gun* section, or even in a bathroom. I was lost among car accessories, clothes, and plants. Lesson number one: German supermarkets are big, American supermarkets are gigantic.

I only planned on buying the most important items to survive the first week: butter, jam, ham, and bread. And there is lesson number two: Bread in Germany is crunchy, sugarless, dark or white, and big, medium, or small. It was an impossible task to find that in the US. Every bread contains sugar and is soft. My frustration led me to the baker who was just about to take out a new batch of freshly baked bread. I asked him to keep one of the pieces of bread in the oven for another fifteen minutes to make sure that it gets crunchy. His expression was priceless. He asked his supervisor whether he was allowed to do that. The supervisor did not know either and called her manager, who approached the scene shortly afterward.

An interrogation begins. Where are you from? What are you intentions with our bread? Why would you want it burned? My accent gives me away, a non-American, just wanting his bread to be crunchy, a novelty. I waited another ten minutes to get the bread and left the bakery. When I got back home, I took out the warm loaf, hoping to bite into a piece of crunchy bread. It is still soft, but I liked it.

"How are you?" In Germany, this question starts a conversation. Upon entering my first American shop, I was immediately asked how I was. At first, I was irritated, asking myself why a stranger would want to know this. I decided to be open to the novelty, so I answered that I was well but overwhelmed because I had just arrived in the US. I told the vendor that I was excited to start my new adventure. She was shocked. She smiled, slowly tiptoed away from me, approached her colleague, and told her all about our encounter. Did I say something wrong? Was I being rude?

The following day, and after a night of contemplation, I was ready to try again. I entered a different shop just to experience the whole situation anew. Upon my entrance, I was asked, "How are you?"

Before I could answer, the person just left, leaving me stranded amidst cultural differences. With frustration gradually boiling up within me, I exited the shop to meet with my American colleague for lunch.

Agitated, I sat down to eat just to find my colleague regarding me and asking, "How have you been doing?" Seismographs could likely detect my inner earthquakes. I begged him to explain to me why Americans keep asking me about my health but disappear. "It is a polite, superficial greeting Americans use." I demanded more explanation. I then learned to just smile and walk the other way too.

I went out to find a post office, since my family loves to receive postcards. I walked, thinking about how I needed to buy some stamps and postcards, and enjoyed wandering around Newark, getting to know my new home. I found myself amongst trees in a park. I continued walking in the attempt to find my way. I took out my phone to try to search for my way back. My phone had no reception.

My last resort: I had to ask someone for help, something that does not come naturally to me.

I approached the first person I saw and asked, "Where is the closest post office?" Of course, it did not occur to me to ask for the Main Street, as a point of direction. The young woman looked at me in awe, hiding her laughter behind her kindness.

"Just cross that small hill and follow this path for another half a mile." I was five minutes north of the nearest post office. I bought three cards and was asked: "How are you?" but this time I understood.

10

People and Places

Ashwini Sansare, India

I still remember the night I left my home country, India, to come to the United States to pursue my graduate studies. With only a few hours to go for my flight, I was a bundle of nerves. My 80-year-old grandmother asked me what was bothering me the most. Was it the coursework that was scaring me? Or was I afraid of losing touch with family and friends? I thought for a moment and replied that it was the idea of living in a country where the people look, talk or dress nothing like me that was making me nervous. She smiled, "That's the thing about people and places! They all seem different at first, but they are really just the same everywhere!" At that time, I didn't believe my grandma. She had never once left the country, what would she know! But in the past few years that I have lived here, I have realized how true her words were! Below are three experiences that made me realize that people are just as humane, open-hearted and kind wherever you go.

My first surprise was on landing at the airport in the US, as I steeled myself for answering the immigration officer's questions. I had heard of people having a tough time at the immigration counter and had begun to think of immigration officers as tough, unbreakable creatures. Officer: "So you are a physical therapist back home?" I answered in affirmative. "What should I do for this muscle pain that I have?" Me (taken aback at the line of questioning): "Neck stretches, strengthening, blah! Blah!". After some routine visa questions, Officer: "How many times do you think I should stretch?" Me: "Looking at how bad your posture is, fifty times!" The officer looks at me in surprise. I remember he still has my passport in his hand and keep my audacity in check. "I mean, you should repeat them as often as possible, maybe hourly". Officer: "Wow, you guys are tough!" With my passport now back in my hand, I walk away smiling, thinking maybe immigration officers are not that bad! And if you are lucky, you can see the more humane side of them! In the past, I have been dragged aside by family and friends back home for free physical therapy consultations at random places, but this one tops my list!

My second story is about my first Thanksgiving in the US. My American landlord had called me over for dinner. She had adopted three kids, who were all deaf and used sign language and lip reading for communication. Despite that, I could see they were laughing and joking like any other siblings would. I was a little apprehensive and shy at first, as this was my first time interacting this closely with an American family. But my landlord made me feel comfortable and asked me about my life back home. As I was telling them about my younger sister, the only daughter pointed to me and said something in sign language. She said "She wants to know your opinion on coloring her hair red or purple. Since you have a younger sister, she thinks you probably are more fashion-savvy than her brothers!" And that's how we both hit it off! I spent the rest of the dinner chatting away with her (with the help of my landlord's translation skills), just the way I would have with my little sister back home. I had a really good time at the dinner and left feeling less lonely in this big country. Over the years, I have realized that Thanksgiving is an intimate family event, and an invitation speaks volumes about how open-hearted, welcoming one can be. That night, my landlord didn't just share her meal with me, she shared her family.

My third story is about the time I decided to visit a popular Indian temple in Pittsburgh, on the occasion of Diwali, an Indian festival. It was located about an hour's drive outside the city and wasn't accessible by public transport. Since I didn't have a driver's license, I took a cab there. I spent about an hour at the temple and decided to call the cab company for a ride back. Somehow, there weren't any cabs available in that area at that time. This was before the days of Uber. I tried for a couple of more hours without any luck and started to panic! I was stuck outside the city, at this temple, with no means of getting home! The security guard, who had just gotten off duty, saw my anguish and offered me a ride home. I was obviously very suspicious of a random stranger. But I did need a ride home. He took me to the reception and had them verify his identity and informed them of his offer to drop me home. He had me call my roommate and gave her his contact and the car number plate as well. When I asked him if my home would be on his way, he said he lived a few minutes away from the temple. So, he drove an hour each way just to drop me home! I was bowled over by the kindness of a stranger, especially towards someone from a foreign country.

The above three stories are just a quick snapshot of the myriad of experiences I have had, meeting and knowing different people in the US. I came to this country expecting people who were, in essence, very different from me. And sure, they look different, and talk with a different accent. But the experiences that were most memorable were also the most familiar and the ones I could relate most easily to. Giving physical therapy consultations at the least expected moments, discussing fashion with my landlord's daughter, experiencing random acts of kindness from strangers... weren't these moments exactly what I would experience back home too? Maybe my grandma was right. Maybe at their core, people and places are the same. They might just look different on the outside!

My New Name is "Practice"

Aishah Moafa, Saudi Arabia

When I lived at home, my life was very easy because I was dependent on others. I would say that in most things that I had to do, related with my daily life, I had the support of my husband and my family. That was because I grew up in a broken family, so I was my mother's everything. She would do anything that I would ask for. After she passed away, I had to ask my husband to help me with my daily duties, such as going shopping and taking care of children. One day, I received an English Language scholarship to study in the United States. It was not easy because I had many problems. The first one was that my husband wouldn't be able to take a leave of absence from work. Therefore, I decided to come with my brother. The second difficulty was that my brother was just 18 years old, meaning that I had to take care of him. Moreover, we have a different mother, so we were not familiar with each other and needed to get to know each other.

In terms of being in the United States, it was my first time traveling to a country that uses English as a primary language. Also, my English was basic at that time. I was not able to drive, and I needed to take care of two children. In the first month, I was too excited to predict the difficulties that I might go through. I was busy with discovering places, friends, cultures, teachers, nature, religions and myself. As the time went by, I started realizing that I had numerous responsibilities. My brother was not able to provide help for my kids or teach me how to drive. The picture of the perfect life that I had imagined turned out to be false, because I only thought about the positive and ignored the potential struggles. I started learning how to drive. I failed the driving test three times, but I passed finally and now I have my driver's license. As time passed, I started learning how to deal with these problems, and how to be independent.

I tried to take every single opportunity to teach my kids knowledge and improve their living skills. Now they can learn by themselves and try to make good use of their free time. There were times that I needed to take my kids to class with me at the English Language Institute. It is stressful, but it is the only way that I could deal with this situation. However, their English kept improving because they practiced and heard English being spoken. About my English, I take every single opportunity to learn; I like to ask people working in the stores how I can pronounce words. Sometimes I ask them for permission to record their voices. I used to come early to class, and sometimes I was the last student to leave. I always had many questions for my teachers. My friends told me that they could hear my voice when they were next to my class. One of my best friends used to call me "Practice" instead of Aishah because whenever we went somewhere, I would stop and talk to people even if we would be late.

Fortunately, I got the IELTS score that I wanted after completing the third session of my English language program. The first person I told was my teacher because I think he was the only one who knew how much I was determined to learn English. He replied, "Your hard work paid off!" I remember days when my friends hung out and they called me to join them; I would tell myself to focus on the reason why you are here and watch an English movie instead. This was a fun way to get used to spoken English and learn something new. As result of my hard work, I got accepted into graduate school to study in my program of choice, cybersecurity.

These concerns were not the only things that I had to care of. Back home, I have a bakery business called Dan Cake House, which I started after I completed my bachelor's degree. However, my dream to come to the US to improve my English and to get my master's degree in cybersecurity was bigger than staying in my country and running my bakery. Although I continue to take care of administrative aspects of the business, such as the budget and customer satisfaction, my business partner is responsible for taking care of the daily functions.

Learning about a new culture and knowing how people overseas live were two of my priorities. Thus, living in the US has taught me that American citizens are very polite and helpful. I have many examples, but I would choose the most important two. One is I remember the day I went to Main Street, and I was having difficulty parking my car. Someone offered me help and parked the car for me. The other time was when I went to Washington DC to attend a meeting with my host sponsor. Something happened to my tire and my kids were with me. I could not do anything. I pulled off and started thinking. Suddenly a woman with her husband stopped by and offered to change my tire. I will never ever forget the help that they gave. Also, I have learned many etiquettes and customs from citizens like holding doors open for other people, smiling, and saying, "Hi."

Finally, I would like to finish up with some advice. Believing in yourself and giving yourself a chance is the key to success. Sometimes I think what if I told myself that day when I got accepted to this scholarship program that "it is hard, and I am not going to make it." Everything would have ended before it started. I hope my story will give students hope that life is exciting and beautiful as we learn and grow through different experiences.

12

How Did You Go About Understanding Local Customs, Traditions and Communication Protocols?

Somi Kim, South Korea

It was a great decision that I made to start my Delaware life with a homestay program. I cannot imagine my life here without my homestay family. Even I can say that the highlight of my English training program was to have the homestay experience. Not only was I able to improve my English, but I could also learn more about American culture and customs, including table manners, traditional dishes, and community work. I have lived with my homestay mom for over six months now. During this time, I have shared everything with her, from the first day of arrival in Delaware to today. Of all these valuable moments, I would like to share a few memories here.

Not long after I arrived here, my homestay mom arranged dinner with her kin: her daughter, her son-in-law, and two grandchildren. She said it was just a family gathering and us having dinner together. We prepared food and drinks and made the table. At first, it looked like a formal western dinner, using a fork and knife. I started recalling what was the right way to use silverware. I felt a little bit awkward. I didn't know how I sneaked into their conversation, and how I should response to their joke. To be honest, at first, I didn't know that was even a joke. So, I just smiled repeatedly. That was the only thing that I could use to show my gratitude for this dinner. It wasn't easy enough to enjoy the dinner for over two hours.

Then, the two children started arguing about the meal. They didn't want to finish their dinner. But because their parents and grandmother, who was my homestay mom, were looking at them and expecting them to finish their meal, they secretly put their chicken on each other's plate and started fighting. Our dinner was finished in yelling and crying aloud. I got tired, even though I didn't talk a lot and ate enough food. However, somehow, I began to feel comfortable and enjoyed this gathering. It was not a formal western gathering anymore, but a close family gathering. I liked the way the kids got along with me, and I liked to watch their fierce but caring conversation with their grandmother. Because this gathering was not formal, I could feel what the general American lifestyle looked like and I could fit into the group as a family member.

Here is another unforgettable moment that I have had with my homestay mom. I am a nurse and had 6 years of work experience. As a nurse, I feel worthwhile when I am helping others. Fortunately, my homestay mom does volunteer work called 'Meals on Wheels', which delivers meals to people who needed help with grocery shopping and access to food. I had a chance to help her. It was a marvelous experience, and it was the moment when the community was brought in my life. I saw how seniors live, and more importantly, how elderly people help each other. That experience wholly changed my prejudiced image of America. My thought toward Americans was mostly occupied with egocentrism, in which Americans could thrive at the highest level of economy and advance in many different fields. However, altruism would be more fit to portray my experience of the American custom. Not only does this experience help me understand the community, but small donation booths on Main Street are also good examples for how people help others in need. At least people in Delaware, no matter how old they are, care for others consciously and for the environment seriously, through small but precious campaigns or movements, such as no straw movement in a bar to save marine creatures. Their lives go along with the poor. Whenever they have a party, they frequently allocate some part of profit for others. I think it is a part of their customs. Thanks to my homestay mom, I was able to see the community itself. This small town is living with not only college students, but also the local neighborhood. They help and flourish with each other. Because of all these reasons, I could not help but love it here.

In conclusion, I could better understand and feel the American culture and customs through my homestay experience. Had I not chosen to stay in a homestay, I would still be confused and would try to find people from my own culture. Homestay has helped me enjoy being around Americans. On top of that, looking around and being involved in the local community is also a decent way to have insight into the community and local customs. It will be much better if I can join the community and devote myself to the work. Basically, the key to my being able to understand their life was to jump into their life. At first you might feel awkward and uncomfortable, but it is normal to feel that way. However, I am sure people around you will welcome you and you will find great hospitality from them as I have.

13

A Gentle Spectacle!

John Wambui, Kenya

Here I was at the beach, a bow-legged, bald-headed, boney kid dressed up in his Sunday best, seated in the midst of a barely clothed crowd watching the tides dancing to the rhythm of the dying summer's afternoon breeze. In Kenya, it was a cultural crime for women to walk around in mini-skirts, yet here I was in Jersey Shore staring at women running around in their star-sparkled bikinis. In Kenya, it was considered a taboo for men to walk around in their underwear. Yet here I was, a young, confused lad trying to decipher whether it was me or the men around me in their striped undergarments who were more disturbed. I was 21 years old when I came to America for school. Back then, I recall, I was carrying a small black luggage in which I had neatly tucked a small white and aqua-blue striped towel, a wrinkled pair of pale-blue jeans, an old white shirt, a toothpaste, an over-used toothbrush, a metallic-silver family photo album, a pair of old white and black sneakers, and a worn out 50-dollar note pinned deep inside my wallet. I was a 5.5 ft. tall, 123lb tiny, boney, bald headed young man with a bloated belly looking forward to a new life in America, as a student.

Back then, everything I knew about America was from the movies and television shows. And as you can imagine, my image of America was thus made up of a fine recollection of beautiful mansions with large blue backyard swimming pools, neatly packaged behind the white picket fences not so far away from the Hollywood's glamorous lifestyle. I imagined young-tattooed men cruising through the boulevards in their big fast cars waving at young women in their star-sparkled bikinis, driving their convertible Porsches with their hair prancing to the tunes of the summers' zephyr. It was indeed a spectacular spectacle - one born of my young naïve imagination.

However, as the summer's breeze began to wane and the sun began to recede into the golden eastern horizons, the fall foliage ushered in a spectacular scenery that was nothing less of a total enchantment. The multi-colored trees whose falling leaves carpeted the boulevards redefined what magic was to me. In Kenya, I was only used to seeing green leaves and trees, yet here I was now gazing at a rainbow of trees! I felt like I was in a mystical land, standing between the spectrum of colors in those tree dotted streets. I was both stunned and enchanted by the blossoming picturesque that covered the boulevards. Within the briefness of the moments, the spectrum of colors and of magic taught me how rare and infinite beauty is indeed-if only for a brief moment! For when I thought I was getting used to the magic, a skeleton holding a butcher's knife popped up on my neighbor's backyard, then a scarecrow dressed up like a grim reaper, and then an adult size doll dressed up like a nurse holding a bloody axe stood by a cracked tombstone! It was Halloween! In my Kenyan state of mind, it was witchcraft! I recall locking myself in my room and calling my friend and telling him, "I think my neighbor is a witch. I can't stay here; I have to go back home!" It took two Halloweens for my friend to convince me that I was not living in a witchcraft infested society! I dressed up like the Phantom of Opera for the fourth Halloween.

In the years to come, I struggled to get accustomed to the American lifestyle. I was scared of many things. I was scared of loneliness. My family and network of friends were all back in Kenya. I was nervous that no one would understand my broken British English dotted with my thick Kenyan accent. I recall struggling to pronounce phrases like the Americans, which often ended in frustrations. It was a terrible frustration trying to pronounce the word 'water' like an American where a 't' sounds like a 'd'! I was afraid that I was never going to fit in among my peers both at home and school.

Back then, I was just a bow-legged, bloated-bellied, and soft-spoken kid who had no idea that in America, 'bathroom and restroom' actually means a 'toilet'. So, I always wondered what it meant when my classmates said they were going to the 'bathroom or restroom' during class hours because in Kenya, bathrooms are places where one goes to take a bath, or a shower, and restrooms are places where people go to rest. It was such a mental dissonance trying to articulate why Americans parked in driveways and drove in parkways! I still recall that feeling the moment I landed in America! It was in 2007. The year of the Pig. The Fire Pig. I felt confused, alone, and lost!

Today, 10 years after, I am still learning the American way of life. I still get lonely even when surrounded by people. I still miss my family, my traditional food, my friends, and my culture. Every time I go to a party, I still feel like the weird kid standing in the corner. In classes, I can still hear my annoying accent reverberating throughout the classroom walls. Sometimes I just wonder whether my classmates can understand me! I still wonder whether my teachers think I am smart enough or I am just an empty coconut shell! I still hear questions, such as "do you guys in Africa eat lions, giraffes, or cheetahs?" And I am still thrilled by those who take curiosity in learning about my culture. In all these years, what I have learned is that you never get used to the American way of life, you just learn to grind along with it. You just learn how to balance the different cultural norms and expectations while allowing yourself to experience the wonders that America can afford you.

14

Long Road to America!

Mehmet Altingoz, Turkey

I had always wanted to study abroad. My government was sending graduate students to the United States to get their post graduate degrees. It is a very long story. The short version is that I worked hard and obtained this scholarship. After countless paperwork, I finally received my visa. Soon after this, the departure day had come. I was sitting in the airplane. It was about to leave for New York. A deep conversation between logical me (italic typing) and overly enthusiastic me (regular typing) began, which continued during the flight.

You needed to do many arrangements before leaving. Do you think you have a good game plan?

Of course, I do!

Let us see. How will you get to Newark, DE from the airport?

After the customs, I will take the AirTrain to Jamaica Station. Then, I will take the long island railroad to Manhattan. Then, I will walk a little bit. Finally, I will take the last Megabus to Newark.

Your flight is delayed half an hour. Due to this delay, it is going to arrive probably half an hour later than the estimated arrival time. Though, if the flight arrived on time, it is very likely that you will miss the Megabus. It does not seem like you have enough time. What if you miss the bus?

Do not worry. I will not miss the bus. I purposely chose a seat by the exit door at the end of the airplane. Therefore, I will be the first person to leave the airplane.

Let us say, a miracle occurred, and you made it on time to the bus. Then what?

My friend will pick me up in Newark.

"Your friend"? You only spoke with him a few times on the phone. In addition, how will you let him know when you are at the bus stop? You do not have a phone.

I will ask a stranger to use their phone.

Without speaking English? I hope you will not be accused of trying to steal a cell phone while you are trying to borrow one. Where will you stay in Newark, if you can ever get there?

Thanks for the good thoughts. My friend might offer his couch.

What if he does not? You do not have money with you. You cannot go to a hotel. Well, even if you had money you would not be able to get a room because you cannot speak ENGLISH!

While logical me and enthusiastic me were having this conversation, I was given a blue form, which I later discovered was the I-94 'Customs Declaration' form. I did not know how to fill it out. While I was looking at it with blank eyes, I fell asleep. Finally, we were done flying over the Atlantic Ocean and I could see pretty landscape, which I thought was the US (I later found out it was Northeastern Canada).

We were about to land. How nice! Wait, I still need to fill out the blue form. I asked the flight crew to help. Their English was poor too. We were having a mini crisis, which I later found very amusing. Upon the extensive collaboration between the flight crew and me, I managed to fill out the form.

Despite the departure delay, the airplane landed on time, at 5pm. It seemed like the pilots made up for lost time in air. This was good news. I could make it on time to the Megabus. However, my exit did not open. I was the last person to leave the airplane since I was at the back and only the front exit opened.

I hurried to the customs. I got there at 5:30pm. There were so many people ahead of me. Finally, at 6:15pm it was my turn. I was nervous that I would not be able to communicate in English with the customs officer. Fortunately, the officer only asked how I was doing and asked for my documents. It took him only a few minutes to go through the documents and approve them.

As soon as I left the US customs area, I saw my suitcases. This was great. I did not lose much time for claiming my luggage. Then, I ran to the AirTrain, while carrying two giant suitcases and a huge backpack. I arrived at Jamaica Station at 6:30pm. It was time to take the Long Island Railroad to Manhattan. There were kiosks around, but I could not figure out how to get a ticket. Fortunately, a train station worker helped me get a ticket. I ran to the train tracks. Arriving there at 6:47pm, I had just missed the train. In addition, the 7pm train had been cancelled. The next train left at 7:15pm. Finally, at 7:50pm, I was in Manhattan. I ran to the bus station. I got there at 8:05pm. The last bus to Newark had left 5 minutes ago.

I told you. (Logical me talks again) I know. Ugh! I asked a stranger if I could use their phone and called my friend. He told me to take a bus to Philadelphia, which I did. When the bus arrived in Philadelphia, he was there. I saw him for first time in my life in person but, at that moment, I could not have been happier. I stayed at his apartment for three days and figured out everything in time.

Since I came to the US, I received a master's degree, a graduate minor, a graduate certificate. I published academic articles, I presented in national academic conferences, and I worked with the World Bank, the Tiffany & Co. Foundation, and many more. Currently, I am a PhD student at the University of Delaware. All started with a little adventure in New York!

To conclude, I want to say a few things to international students who are planning to study in the U.S.

Do not worry. Just do your best and everything will work out for you!

***** 🪕

15

Highways? No Way!

Edgar Salazar, Colombia

I am going to open my heart and tell you that I have always hated driving; even the bumper cars at the county fairs make me feel that my life is under serious risk. To be honest, one of my goals in life is to have enough money to buy a fancy car and hire a 24-hour driver, just for me. I would have never imagined that coming to the US was going to force me to face my unjustified aversion to cars.

When I received my acceptance letter from the University of Delaware, I was honestly thrilled and, after telling my whole family about the good news, my wife and I had a long conversation, where basically we promised ourselves to do our best to adapt to the American lifestyle. We watched a lot of YouTubers talking about their experiences and the Top 10 things you should or should not do in the US. The first advice they always said was to start creating a credit record. As somebody told me once, "you are no one if you do not have a credit card". Well, that was not difficult. There are many options for international students; you just need to go online a make some clicks. The second biggest advice anyone mentioned was to get a driver's license as soon as the airplane lands. "That can't be true!" I said, "In *How I met your mother*, Lilly, Marshall and even Barney take the train; this YouTuber is trying to make us buy a car, he is probably a car dealer". "Don't be a chicken and let's go to get an international driver license", my wife said. "Well, I could, but I really think these guys from YouTube are messing with us; nowadays, any fool can upload a video". At the end, I refused to get the license in my home country, hoping that all what I watched in *How I met your mother* was true.

The first months here in Newark were actually amazing. I remember seeing Main Street for the first time and saying to myself: "There is no way I will get bored here; I don't know why Americans buy a car if everything you need is in a single street". But, as time passed, I started to think that maybe there was something cooler than the half price Mondays burgers at Kates. Don't get me wrong, Kates is delicious, but when you already ate the whole options in the menu, it is time to explore new lands. Deep in my heart I knew that we were missing a lot, and the only way to get in touch with the American culture was buying a car. "We must buy a car as soon as possible, but you'll drive it", I told my wife; "Are you serious, if we buy a car, we both should drive it, no excuses", she said; "I'll drive it if you teach me". Then the adventure began.

Luckily for me, my wife is even a better driver than the bold guy from 'Fast and Furious'. She has over 8 years of driving experience (in manual car) in La Paz, the chaotic and stressful capital city of Bolivia. The first time I took the wheel, it was a nightmare. I did not have the control of the car and I was constantly confusing the brake and the gas pedal; "Just stop or you are going to make us crash", and that was the end of the first lesson. Ten lessons later, I finally could go out from the neighborhood and took the enormous risk to go to the grocery store, two blocks away from home. "Try to be calm and do not forget to sign the turns", my wife said; "Ok, ok do not treat me like a baby", I yelled at her. To welcome me to the roads, one driver beeped the horn like 100 times because I did not sign my left turn. Two months after I started the driving lessons, I was confident and thought I was ready for the test. My wife reminded me that we have not even started yet; I was doing a good job, but I did not know how to park or parallel park. "Parallel what?"; that was my true reaction.

Even for drivers who have been driving for a long time, parallel parking can be a painful experience. You can find videos on YouTube of people trying to parallel park for hours, without achieving it. I thought that everything was over for me and that I would never get my license. "No way, you can do it, you have improved a lot and I won't let you quit, let's work", my wife cheered me up; "That's why I love you, let's do it", I told her. The same day, we were trying to parallel park behind an unknown car. I think we did it ten times and all of them were awfully wrong; at the 11th time, the owner of the car went out and yelled: "Hey, what are you doing to my car"; "push the gas pedal and let's go, now!", my wife said; "Look at us, we are like Bonny and Clyde", "Do not talk while we escape", she answered back.

This story is not over. I already passed the written DVM test. To be honest it was not that difficult. However, the driving test is on the 31st of October. Usually I am not superstitious, but what are the odds of you having the driving test the same day all the spirits, zombies and demons go out to scare people? I am actually thinking about the chance to wear a Jeff Gordon costume that day. "Once you pass the test, you will be ready to drive on highways, but keep in mind that your speed should not be less than 65 mph", my wife said: "Well darling I'll try my best to pass the test, but driving on highways? No way!"

16

The Sandwich Conundrum

Chamath Chandrasekera, Sri Lanka

I still have vivid memories of clambering up the front steps of my dorm, my arms laden with two heavy suitcases, trying not to appear as though I had taken three flights and a Greyhound bus to get there. Nonetheless, I was thrilled to be in the US, fulfilling my dream of pursuing my higher education here. My first dose of culture shock hit me that same day when I was ordering a sandwich from Subway and the employee asked me what kind of bread I wanted. In Sri Lanka, where I come from, they usually don't give you the option of choosing your bread. Reading my puzzled look, the Subway employee motioned to their bread menu. I was unaccustomed to this level of customizability in my sandwiches and I was also increasingly aware of how I was holding up the line. The result was an ill-advised combination of ingredients in my sandwich and me running to my dorm to frantically google how to order a sandwich at Subway!

This was five years ago when I first began my journey as an international undergraduate student in the US. The culture shock which overwhelmed me at first has diminished, but I still encounter moments of it. I am now beginning my graduate studies at the University of Delaware, and I find that I am now in a community that allows me to embrace my identity as an international student, and still integrate with the larger school community.

At the University of Delaware, I had the opportunity to take a summer program for international teaching assistants, where I met graduate students from a host of different countries. I learned some of the cultural mores and biases of students like me from all across the globe. This made me realize how international students bring unique perspectives and opinions, promote cultural awareness, and make the educational experience more interesting and I was grateful to be a part of it. More importantly I savored the chance to indulge in the culinary traditions of my fellow international students. A group of Chinese friends of mine invited me to a hot pot dinner, which is a Chinese fondue-type meal consisting of a simmering pot of broth, with raw meats and vegetables placed around it so people can add and cook whatever they like. It was a completely different dining experience and a fun social activity that I would definitely recommend. My fellow international students and I visited places that we had never visited before, like New York and Washington D.C., often times with American friends. Through programs like this, UD has helped me connect with both international and American students.

One thing I may never escape is the routine onslaught of questions I get about what Sri Lanka is like. Is it a lot like India? Do you eat the same food and celebrate the same holidays? I try to explain how Sri Lanka is a tropical island paradise, rich in culture and history. I also try not to be irked when people think

India and Sri Lanka are similar because we are neighbors. Instead, I patiently explain how different Sri Lanka is from India in terms of its culture, customs, religions and food. After all, promoting awareness of my culture is part of my responsibility as an international student, so I see this as an opportunity to do that.

There are also more practical differences between Sri Lanka and America which requires adjustments from time to time. Public transit varies strikingly and while it is easy to get around Sri Lanka without a car, it is not so easy in America. On the flipside, driving in America is much easier with the vast highways and the absence of cows occasionally wandering on the road! For the first few years here, I struggled without a car. I had friends who were willing to drive me around which was immensely helpful. Experiences like this taught me that a strong support system is vital to an international student's success. In America I learned to connect with people of all backgrounds and personalities, which is something I never had to do in Sri Lanka.

I still face some of the same difficulties I had when I first arrived, although things have become easier with time and experience. Navigating subjects like taxes and healthcare in the US. is always challenging but I am encouraged to learn that Americans find these equally painful to deal with. Adapting to the varying climate in the US was also totally new to me since Sri Lanka sits on top of the equator and has no seasons. Even though Americans often complain about how hot it gets during the summer or how cold it gets during the winter, the weather in Sri Lanka can impact daily living. I am used to conditions including severe drought, resulting in electricity and water cuts, and monsoon seasons where it rains for weeks on end bringing floods and mosquitoes in its aftermath. I have not experienced a Delaware winter yet, so I am really hoping I don't eat my own words!

The struggles of an international student in America are real. The compulsion to convert everything from American dollars to your home currency can leave you feeling abysmally poor or dangerously rich, depending on where you are from. Hearing that employers are allergic to the words "visa sponsorship" can undermine your confidence. The notion that you are under a microscope and any tiny infraction will result in you getting deported can make you feel distressed. In my experience, these problems are often exaggerated and the result of not belonging in a safe space. I have found that the UD community embraces international students and provides a safe space. Here we can build relationships, be treated with equality, follow our passion, and make full use of our talents. We have the freedom to choose our path. It is all about customizing your experience just like with a sandwich!

17

From Lost to Found in Translation

Xueyao Liang, China

Before I departed for the US, I constantly pictured myself at the moment I land in the country. That excitement led to some unrealistic thoughts, such as picturing myself walking out of the plane and kissing the ground. Despite all the concerns poured into my head by my parents, I never felt so certain and prepared for this significant chapter of my life. After all the imagination and curiosity, I left my sheltered home, carried my big suitcase, and walked into the Departure Gate waving to my proud parents. I teared up when I said "Zaijian" to my mom ("goodbye" in Chinese). Then the sadness from the send off moment was soon replaced by hopes and promises. After fourteen hours of flying, I finally arrived in the land of freedom and opportunity. Yet, the reality of a new culture and language soon hit me like a storm. The transformation from being a dragon to a Blue Hen (UD's mascot) has been filled with surprises, sadness, laughter, confusions, understanding and finally embracing.

The first storm that hit me took place in Saladworks on main street. I figured I wouldn't need to say much in a place like this. I kept my order simple, as I was afraid of speaking English. When I finished my order, the lady looked at me and asked "Dressing?" Right away I looked at my clothes, then I realized this might not be what she meant…it was so bizarre for someone to ask about my "dressing" when I simply wanted to purchase a salad. So, I just nodded. "Dressing???" The lady finally had to point her finger to the dressing bars. Then she tried again, "Now here, point to me which one you want?" Despite my strong feeling of embarrassment, I learned my first new word "salad dressing".

Ever since the "Dressing" incident, I became very aware of every word I hear from people. I often ask my American classmates "So why do you say this?" or "Why do you call it that way?" Most of the time, they are not able to provide an answer as English to them is so natural. Once, a girl in my World History class asked if I wanted to "Hang out" sometime. I was beyond confused, since it was not the first time, I ever heard Americans use this term to each other. I finally asked her "Why do people here like hanging themselves so much, and like to do it with someone else? What fun is that?" She immediately burst into laughter and explained to me what the term really means. With laughter, explanation and understanding, I survived my second storm.

As months passed, my world has been broadened as never before. I came to realize that so many stereotypes I had about Americans were not true. For example, Americans don't eat hamburgers or steaks every day, and there are various dining options on and off campus. What impressed me the most about students at UD is everyone I meet has a great sense of curiosity towards my country and culture. At the beginning, I felt quite shocked by so many American students asking me questions, like "Do you have McDonalds in China?" They were even more shocked with my answer: "Oh yeah, it also has 24 hours' home delivery."

My hometown, Guangzhou, is known for its eating culture. One of our famous dim-sum dishes is chicken feet. It apparently isn't an appealing dish to my American friends. Chicken feet is understandably considered something "disgusting" here. The first time they learned about the dish was rather amusing. One of my classmates invited me and a few other students to her house for dinner. She asked, "Would you guys like chicken fingers for dinner?" I, along with the other American girls, said "sounds great!". No one at the moment would have thought what I was picturing in my mind. When I heard "chicken finger", I immediately thought it was the delicious chicken feet. I was quite impressed by my classmates' taste since I did not think most Americans could stand eating chicken feet. When I walked to the dinner table and saw a pile of yellow strips, I once again realized I had wrongly interpreted the word. Everyone laughed when I explained to them what I was thinking.

That night, we talked and laughed for hours about all the things I misinterpreted when I arrived in this country. I was also surprised by how much I didn't know about "my culture", when the students asked me about something like "Duck sauce" or "Fortune cookies". When they told me there is always a little note within the fortune cookies, with message of good luck or some positive sayings, I looked so terrified and they had to ask if I was feeling OK. I sighed heavily and said, "Oh no…when I went to the Chinese restaurant, I ate the whole thing." With endless laughter and stories, I felt closer to these wonderful students, who I am now pleased to call my friends. I also felt closer to this culture and slowly became a Chinese Blue Hen.

The journey of being a Blue Hen has been the greatest blessing in my life. From knowing nothing about the State of Delaware to now becoming a die-hard fan of Wawa and Brew Haha! coffee shop. From the constant struggle of adjusting to cultural and language differences to holding lengthy conversations with professors and friends. This has been a journey filled with everyday surprises. I was once lost in this culture and missed home constantly, yet I found that in opening myself, I allow others to learn from me, as I learn from them. The experience has enriched my life. I now proudly sleep in my UD pajamas and call myself a real "Blue Hen".

18

American Wonder!

Ugochukwu Nsofor, Nigeria

I hail from the eastern part of Nigeria, the Igbo tribe. Going to the University, a feat neither of my parents had the opportunity to accomplish, was quite challenging. So you will agree with me that having my graduate studies in the United States is quite an amazing accomplishment. Before setting out to the United States for my graduate studies, I had anticipated an adventurous experience. The fact that I will be traveling outside the shores of my country for the first time made me even more excited. No doubt, this was going to be a very significant 5-year span of my life. So far, it has been remarkable in every sense.

On arriving at the University of Delaware, I was stunned by its beauty and rich history. I was fascinated by the way the school integrates with its host community, in such fashion that it appears the school flows naturally into the community. There were no boundaries or demarcations. The very fact that you could be on Main Street and be steps away from the campus shows how much emphasis the university places on the need to balance work and life. That was a good first impression of my new home, indeed. But there was more to come, as acclimatizing to my new environment turned out to be more than I had anticipated.

Before coming to America, I have always had the conviction that I possess a very good command of English language. But to my own chagrin that doesn't seem to be the case. I could barely understand the immigration officers at JFK airport. In fact, I think they had more problems making sense of my spoken English. It was a bit embarrassing for me having to repeat my response over and over again just to convey a simple meaning. I noticed with dismay the gradual decline in my desire to engage in conversations in a bid to cover up my recently discovered flaws in spoken English. Overtime, I made friends with some native speakers, who had the patience to filter my speech for clarity and meaning. Hanging out with them these passing years has really improved my ability to enunciate and comprehend words better. Also, I learned that it's more expedient to use American argots when communicating with Americans. For example, I almost ruined a friendship when I told a friend that his mum's booth was messy, when referring to his mum's car trunk, which actually looked untidy. But he thought I was referring to his mum's butt. Thank goodness, I was able to remedy that situation. Now I just say trunk.

My first class at UD was quite remarkable, although filled with anxiety and anticipation, as I had no clue what to expect. The classroom was obviously well selected to match the class size. This was contrary to my undergraduate experience in my home country. Everything seemed well organized and the faculty displayed in-depth knowledge and devotion to their profession. They showed up on time, and if for some reasons were unable to make a class, we were informed before time and were kept busy with homework. The pace of the classes was quite fascinating, as there was so much material to cover in every course. From weekly homework to individual presentations every fortnight, to quizzes every month and midterms, it was indeed a marathon experience that drained the faculty themselves. As if the marathon learning experience and the language barrier was not challenging enough, winter came knocking cruelly.

Initially, I had eagerly anticipated the winter because I wanted to experience snowfall. Little did I know that such experience would come at the expense of five months of freezing temperatures. My so-called winter jackets and fur-coats were acquired with my prior notion of cold weather. Needless to say, they offered no real warmth against the cold. I had to master the art of layering and never to leave the house without a coat during months that are spelt with an 'R' (i.e., September to April). By the next winter, I was well prepared to withstand -35F while on vacation in Wyoming. Nevertheless, I still have a strong nostalgia for the all-year-round summer temperatures that wears the face of sub-Saharan Africa.

One other interesting experience was getting my taste buds receptive to the menu at American restaurants. American cuisines were far off from typical Nigerian or African food. For a while, I had to struggle with the food and my bowels would rumble after eating chili or bread smeared with sweet potatoes and cheese. Ordering at restaurants was really a big deal. My meals were always a surprise because most times I had no clue of what I ordered until it was served. I learned to stick with burgers because no matter how ingenious the caterer wants to be, I am sure to find bread and some meat inside. Having lived here for a while now, I can say that I am pretty much comfortable eating a wide range of food.

Joining social and religious groups on campus have aided my transition into American culture. Through diverse activities that foster interaction and opportunity of meeting new people, I have been exposed to life in America. I had the opportunity of celebrating Thanksgiving and watching the Super Bowl with an American family, though I only understood touchdowns the whole time. I also served as a volunteer during the Pope's visit to Philadelphia and got involved in lots of other activities that aided my integration process. I am very much convinced that these experiences have broadened my views and thought process in so many ways and would positively influence my judgement in the future.

19

From the Dirt Roads of Honduras to the Red Brick Walks of UD

Kervin Zamora, Honduras

The University of Delaware (UD) is truly an amazing place. I feel privileged to be part of this community that is now my home. The Student Centers have become my dining room, the front lawn my back yard, my classmates, my friends, and my host family, my family. Professors became my mentors and my inspiration; they taught me philosophy, history, policy, astronomy, Portuguese, leadership, economics, etc. What can I say about the campus? It is simply beautiful! The red bricks, the mixture of old with new architecture, the amazing trees on the green and the countless colorful spring flowers across campus. UD is a four-season paradise. Whether it is red/orange/yellow in the fall, white in winter, or green with pink and white flowers against blue skies in the spring and summer, UD mesmerizes. But it is the heart of its people that impresses the most.

I am a proud and happy Blue Hen. However, these feelings took a little time to develop in me. UD and the US overall are very different from Honduras. Notice that I said different, not better or worse. For you to understand this difference, I need to mention a thing or two about Honduras and the Latino culture. Honduras is a tropical country, with summer weather all year round. Life in Honduras is happy and simple.

Latinos are generally very warm people. We love to hug, kiss, and talk. In fact, we love those things a little bit too much sometimes. We are passionate, family oriented, and alive overall—we love being social, dancing, music, and soccer. Oh, we also like tortillas, rice, and beans, a lot!

During my first few days in the US, I am not going to lie, I made a few mistakes. I was introduced to a girl, and I gave her a hug and a kiss on her cheek. I soon realized that this was not okay. She turned red. My American friend, instead of helping her understand, allowed me to drown in my embarrassment with his comment and laughter: "Ohhh dude, we don't do that here!" At least, I learned right away that Americans did not like to be kissed or hugged like my buddies in Honduras. Then we went to a restaurant and discovered that they did not have rice, beans, or tortillas. What was I going to eat now!

Well, I was in America after all, so I ordered a burger. I failed to say "well done" when I ordered. I didn't know that that was a thing. In Honduras, when you order food, meat will always be well done. I discovered that many Americans liked eating food on the raw end of the scale. With time, I discovered that when you said, "well done," they actually would cook it through.

I soon learned that the way I pronounced "beach" sounded like a bad word. So, my friends taught me how to say it the correct way. I discovered that when

Americans say, "how are you?", they mean more like "Hello!" One day, someone said "how are you?" to me, and I spent like ten minutes describing my day and my feelings. Soon I realized that he wanted to leave because he kept glancing at his watch. After all this social awkwardness, winter came and yes, I was not well prepared! What do you mean, this would last like four months!? I got used to it with time though, and it was even fun to play in the snow. Dancing at a party was another awkward experience. I was used to my Merengue and Salsa. I was not prepared for the American style. Don't even get me started on dating and asking girls on a date—a completely different game. But like anything, with practice, one improves. With my host family and friends' help, I learned to speak better English and to be socially acceptable in the American world. That included not commenting about people's weight or income, which in Honduras are all fair game.

I realized that I needed to adapt. I had to stop treating the US like Honduras because it was not Honduras. And I had to better understand the American culture. If I was to become a guest in this country, I wanted to know the rules and norms. But I loved my culture. I love being Latino and every single thing that that word means. Was I supposed to give up my culture? I learned that I did not have to. America and UD are full of welcoming, loving people. I learned to coexist as a Latino in the American world. In fact, it became fun and educational to share with my American family and friends the differences between Honduras and the US. This was also productive in classes, in which they valued international input in many class conversations. I went from an awkward guy to a fun and cool foreigner.

Today, awkward moments are rare, because I have become an Americanized Latino, which is not a bad thing. The way I look at it is that I got the best of both worlds. I teach Americans about my culture, and when I go home, I teach my family about the American world. I love the University of Delaware and its people, because I would not be who I am today without their love and support. To all those new international students who come from all over the world, believe me, I understand how much you have given up in order to be here. Nevertheless, I will also tell you that this is the best decision that you have made, because this place is transformational and inspiring. The lessons learned and friendships made here today will shape the person you are tomorrow. UD has given me so much and that is why I can truthfully say, I am a proud and happy Blue Hen.

20

The Broad Horizon

Ashish Chouhan, India

"No stray dogs or cows, SWEET!" Having grown up seeing these animals in India, more on the streets than any other place, these were my first thoughts when I first landed here and peeked out the window of the cab to get the glimpse of what US had to offer.

I first came to UD in the summer of 2014 as a visiting scholar, and that was the first time I was stepping out of my home country, all by myself. I always dreamt of traveling the world, making friends of different nationalities, speaking multiple languages and what not. Getting an invitation letter from UD to spend my summers there was the very first step towards living that dream. The experience I got from those few months and the extent to which I liked this place compelled me to come back here to pursue my graduate studies.

"Yes, I eat beef…" even before I could finish the sentence, she exclaimed, "Awww, but cow is considered as one of the gods in India and everyone worships it, how can you eat beef, dude?" Questions like these kept increasing as I met more and more new people. I try to give an appropriate answer every time, to people who don't know much about other countries and who want to know what my country was like and how were the people, what they do, how they think etc.

Someone asked me once if I ever faced a situation of confusion. Well, if I could tell him one. I will never forget one of the moments when I experienced the so called 'culture shock', when I was invited to play football, and being an actual FOOTBALL fan, I agreed. The next day I hit the field and I saw them playing some sort of game which looked similar to rugby and was nowhere close to football. Later, they told me that this was American football and what I was thinking was called soccer. It still makes me smile when I recall that incident.

What I've learnt here is that there are small things that can make a difference. Kind gestures that we might never notice can say hundreds of words. Holding doors for people, vehicle drivers waiting for pedestrians to pass by, greeting some stranger a good day with a picture-perfect smile, whom you don't even know and many more. Such are the acts I see daily which always put a smile to my face.

It gives me a sense of belonging when I look around in my class and see students just like me and you, from various parts of the globe, so diverse, thousands of miles away from their family, overcoming hundreds of difficulties, be it the language or their beliefs, or the cultural barriers, and still working hard towards achieving the dream for which they were here. I get inspiration, not from some Hollywood celebrity, but from people like these.

Back in India, this is the time when we have all the festivals lined up and we get so many vacations to celebrate. Now that I am here, I hear more of Halloween, Thanksgiving and Christmas and how people start preparing for them well in advance. I am particularly excited about Halloween, but I still need to figure out what I want to be: A knight from Game of Thrones (who would put every other knight to shame because of being too skinny) or an Avenger or Goku. Ahhh, this is more stressful than studying for a mid-term.

One of the many things I like the most about UD is the weekly coffee hours, organized by the Office for International Students and Scholars, where we get to meet new people and make friends. I am very lucky to have utilized this opportunity to make so many friends from all round the globe. An American friend, who always introduces himself as a person who lives on the street of Six Flags, to an Australian brother, who never forgets flashing his national flag wherever he travels. From a Sri Lankan buddy to one of my best friends from Swaziland. Never in my life had I ever imagined that someday I would learn Turkish with the help of some of the most generous and friendly Turks. Just a few months and I have had the time of my life here.

I have become a huge fan of Mexican food, Spanish language, American games and Chinese names (and they are still hard to pronounce and remember). My taste buds have developed a liking for burritos and tacos. Bailando is now one of my favorite Spanish songs, even though I don't know the meaning of most of its lyrics. I have started following Football (yes, American football and not soccer) and sometimes I even have difficulty recalling whether this person was Xin or WanXin. But in spite of this, I am learning to live in a community full of diverse but amazing people.

The overall experience of being in the US has been terrific. I have learned how to overcome different challenges that life would put in our path. The biggest has been learning how to cook, with which I still struggle. I feel the experience I've had here has transformed me into a person more responsible and who is ready for any kind of situation. One thing I myself have learned is to get out of my comfort zone, because as they say 'life begins at the end of your comfort zone.'

21

The Missing Suitcases: A Metaphor of My Life at UD

Hanna Olsson, Sweden

Every avid airplane-traveler's worst nightmare is to have their suitcases go missing. The fear of your most valuable belongings being lost, the fear of having to haphazardly buy all of the necessities you might need in order to survive your vacation. My "vacation" is supposed to last for four years. As stated in the majority of the major airlines' policy, they are responsible for your luggage once it's checked in and will replace the costs of your belongings if by chance it would get lost. Not so bad, you might think; getting some cash to replace your old, ragged clothes with some new ones. In theory, this might sound wonderful, but in reality, as a jetlagged Swedish girl all alone in a foreign country, it is not idealistic.

As an international student from Europe, getting to the University of Delaware (UD) by airplane is a no-brainer. So, like every eager freshman, I filled up my two suitcases with everything I might possibly need to survive my 4 years at the University. I had everything planned out, everything: From how I was going to get to the airport to where I was going to stay my first night in the US. After spending a great amount of time flying across the Atlantic, I finally arrived in Philadelphia, only to find that my suitcases were not there. At the time, this seemed like my worst nightmare, but I survived.

Sure, I may not have been looking all that fashionable walking around in an oversized UD t-shirt I was given for free during my first day, but at least I had something to wear. Sure, the people who saw me in the communal bathrooms using only complimentary sample-sized toiletries from the airport may not have gotten the best first impression of me, but they learnt not to make assumptions too quickly, once I told them my story. Sure, the stores of Main Street may not have provided the greatest selection of everyday essentials, but they were my savior until I befriended Americans who were willing to help an international student out by driving them to the closest Target. Losing my suitcases made me see the US and its mindset for what it really was; not judgmental but instead open-minded, not narcissistic but instead widely generous, and definitely not conceited but instead extremely supportive. I realized that I entered this university, this state, even this country, with an already made-up presumption of how the US functioned, much of it based on my annoyance caused by the missing suitcases. The response I got from people during this mild crisis completely blew away my mind, and my presumptions. I learned that people and things aren't always what they seem, and that first impressions are not to be trusted. The girl who commented on my XXL t-shirt later helped me carry bag after bag of groceries to my dorm, and the girl who stared me down for using a perfume sample out of a magazine later offered me a toothbrush and toothpaste. Individuality is embraced. People's struggles are aided, and a community-sense is what's being strived for. The only egoistic ideal in the American mindset was the one set by my presumptuous expectations.

"Missing" became a keyword for my first week at the University of Delaware. Besides the suitcases, I realized that my name was missing from many of my professor's class lists, I realized that my roommate who was supposed to move in on the same day as me was nowhere to be found, and I realized that the Swedish flag was missing from the majestic International flag display in Trabant Student Center. Somehow, all of these puzzle-pieces that represented my life at UD were missing, and I really didn't understand why. Eventually, everything worked out: On the updated class lists my name appeared, my roommate moved in two days later, and I was promised a Swedish flag in Trabant for the Spring semester, but the initial question still remained.

In hindsight, I think I'm grateful that the suitcases went missing. Why? The situation I was put in forced me to get out of my comfort zone, to ask for help, to make new friends. Isn't that what freshman year is supposed to be all about? The suitcases also became a scapegoat for all of my worries. Instead of worrying about finding the location of my first class, I could worry about finding a place that sold towels so I could actually take a shower. They became a visual representation of everything that was wrong in my life, making me believe that any problem henceforth being a piece of cake.

Did I ever retrieve my suitcases you may wonder? I did, eventually. By that time, I had come to terms with all of these "missing" parts of my life. My suitcases may have been missing, my name may have been missing, my flag may have been missing, and even my roommate may have been missing, but at least I was here. The puzzle-pieces of my life were lost, so I created an entire new puzzle. I stopped trying to fill in the blanks that represented my expectations of the US, and instead just drew a whole new picture. The missing suitcases were a metaphor for finding myself; a 19-year-old international student all alone in a foreign country. I was just like the suitcases: undetermined, uncharted, missing. I had to come to terms with the fact that the suitcases, and I, may never really be found. But once the suitcases were returned and restored, so was I. I got to a major realization: The suitcases, and myself, may have been missing, but they were never truly lost.

22

You are Russian!

Olga Parshina, Russia

"What? You don't drink vodka? How come? So, do you ride bears instead of cars in your country? No, don't tell me you are cold. You must like this weather. You are Russian!"

This is the usual set of questions I got when I arrived in the US a year ago and met new people every day. Seriously, I even had a standard list of replies in my head, that I learned by heart, in order to save me some time. But I was incredibly excited to answer these questions each time because I realized that I got into a brand-new world, where people do not know anything about me and about my life back across the ocean. The understanding that I also knew very little about people and culture here came quite fast.

The first thing that struck me was that I could easily understand what my professors were discussing in the classroom, but too often I had no idea what my new friends were talking about. "Hey, what's up? Hyped for the weekend? Wanna hang out tonight? You'll nail it, don't freak out. Okey dokey, see ya then! Seriously? Would you be so kind to say that again for me and a bit slower, please? Why on earth did I spend 15 years of my life studying English not to understand a word of what people my own age are saying to me?

Don't worry, this goes away pretty fast, especially if you spend a lot of time with your friends like I did. Soon enough I was just killing it! One might ask where I found the opportunity to make so many new friends outside the classroom. Well, I was extremely lucky to be accepted particularly to UD because our University has one of the best college swing dance clubs on the east coast! What is swing dance? It is when you improvise to jazz music with your dance partner whom you might have never seen before. And UD does it and does it wonderfully! Just in a week after my arrival, I had already travelled to Baltimore and Philadelphia with the club to dance with new people! In two weeks, I found myself in Philadelphia getting my first medals in dance competitions! In three weeks, I was helping to teach in the club, which of course helped me to gain a lot of confidence and a feeling that I was needed (this is extremely important!). But actually, it doesn't matter what kind of activity you choose to do. The key is not to hide behind closed doors. There is, maybe, still a bit foreign to me, but such a wonderful world outside! Especially if it doesn't snow here.

Yes, I am from Russia, but what is wrong with you, Delaware? Why do you have such a rough winter? Although it was so amusing when it was 5 degrees Fahrenheit (this is another whole topic for jokes: try to cook the pie in the oven at 150 degrees Fahrenheit because you forgot to convert to Celsius!) and everybody was touching my fluffy Russian winter coat and I saw they were envious. Also, what a joy to have classes cancelled when there was a light snowfall outside! It was a real shock for me and one more reason to make fun of my American friends who were clearly suffering from terrible weather conditions. When they asked me what to do to warm themselves up, I would say: "drink hot tea (not vodka!) and eat a hot home-cooked meal." And here comes another surprise. We do have different eating traditions.

You really don't have to cook anything in America. Almost everything is already done for you. The grocery stores here have an excessive amount of prepared food to offer. I remember wandering between shelves at the grocery store and wondering how much food a human being needs for life. Also, sometimes really unusual ingredients are mixed inside the meal: salad with lettuce, apples, strawberries and bacon? Sure. As a friend of mine (American) said: "To sell this salad to an American, you have to put bacon inside."

Well, all this is about living in a new environment. But as a student, I also had some surprises to encounter in the classroom and on campus. First, the University is amazingly beautiful! I always wanted to feel how it is to study in a castle-like buildings, like in the Harry Potter movies! Some would question my judgment now, but these people should see how campus buildings are designed in another country (like mine). Nothing as exciting, believe me. Furthermore, the University provides excellent facilities such as gyms, food courts and libraries. There were days when I stayed in our library till 2 am because it is an excellent place to study. And to sleep.

One of the unusual things about the studying process in the US for me was individualism and overall control during the semester. In Russia, we often study in the groups and we are really open to share the ideas about homework with classmates. Here it is more about individual progress and knowledge. Also, you have to be focused during the whole semester in order to succeed. No worries, constant deadlines, midterms and quizzes will keep you in shape. I think it is really crucial to know these facts about higher education in America to be prepared.

All that being said, I want to conclude by saying that studying at UD and being an international student is a wonderful opportunity to explore the world, to widen your horizons and to break stereotypes. Each day you find something new. Yes, there are some moments when you have to be flexible and adjust, but isn't this ability a sign of a mature person? I spent a year and half at UD, and I can tell that my world has changed a lot: I learned so much, I have so many new friends and I finally fell in love. I even can put bacon in his strawberry salad.

23

Newark: A Cozy Home to Keep Us Together

Byron Acosta, Colombia

The very first time I got off the plane, a smiling airport officer looked at me and said, "My wife always says: Why do so many people come to America? Don´t they realize that we live in an asylum?" Those words really initially disturbed me. "What am I doing here!" I thought. Of course, I knew he was just pulling my leg, but inside, I was suddenly very conscious that I was about to live in a place with totally different customs, which wasn´t going to be an easy task. Not just the customs, but how I could get by in a place with a completely different language, manners, weather and culture from mine? Well, it would certainly be a long and fraught road ahead. However, it was definitely a worthwhile decision. After all, the United States is a place where immigrants overcame incredible hardships no matter how difficult they may have appeared. Because of that, living as a foreigner so far away from home has been like climbing a mountain. It can be physically and mentally challenging, but easier if you have the right equipment and inspirational support. The best path to get beyond living abroad is not to be afraid of learning the language, overcoming prejudices and finding out the advantages hidden at first sight.

As a newcomer, I hoped to internalize the language without fear of confusion or linguistic cultural misunderstandings. When I began living in Newark, I heard someone to say, "What a beautiful day, TGIF!" Sounds good, I thought, and I started to use that expression following everything. "What a delicious food, TGIF! What a wonderful movie, TGIF!" Obviously, some guys teased me every time I said that but, I thought that it was because of my accent. A good soul finally set me straight by enlightening me on the actual meaning of TGIF: "Thank God It´s Friday." How embarrassing!

On another occasion, while debating with some friends about politics. I said, "Sorry, on the topic of politics, I am "septic"." I spent ten minutes trying desperately to convey that I wanted to say I am a "skeptic", but of course, my effort was in vain. They mocked me the whole afternoon. These misunderstandings have become part of my natural process of learning English, one that I now confess to actually enjoy. If we want to adapt to another country, we shouldn´t be afraid of making mistakes, which is the best way to learn.

Who doesn´t have prejudices about other countries, other people, and other cultures?

Perhaps everybody has pre-conceived notions about the unknown. Before coming to Newark, I thought that Americans were ethnocentric. That they didn't look outside their own borders. That they watched TV all day and ate junk food.

I was acting like a grumpy old man, confined in a house without windows. Nonetheless, my first evening with my American Homestay family was spent talking about food, music and cultures from around the world. We even danced Salsa and ate Indian food! As time went by, I shared time with a lot of locals, and I gradually realized that I was very wrong about my previous idea about "The lazy American". The reality opened my mind and I found out that the United States is not a place with one culture; it is where many kinds of cultures are embraced and coexist.

Every place in the world, no matter how small, has enormous advantages which are frequently hidden. During my first week living in Newark, I heard some students say that living here was boring. To be honest, at the beginning I thought the same. What could be interesting in a place with only one Main Street, a few businesses and a sizable university campus? Well, I found out that those characteristics are precisely what make living here advantageous. If the people live close to each other, you tend to run into them pretty frequently.

This is like a friend told me "A small house keeps the family together." Well, I have to say that I wholeheartedly agree! Newark is a cozy home where everybody is nearby, and because of that, you can find someone to share your hobbies with! When I understood this, I noticed how many groups are in Newark. There are sports clubs, book clubs, music clubs and many others. Do you want to make films or to learn to dance? Do you want to play video games or go hiking? There are all kinds of clubs for every kind of hobby. There is even those who enjoy dressing up like medieval knights and simulate fights with weapons! It´s amazing! In order to adapt to a new home, we need to take advantage of the particular features that a place provides, and Newark has my favorite one: keeps the community together.

Living as an international student in Newark, I learnt to enjoy my language mistakes, to face my own prejudices and to appreciate the warm community life. As a Colombian, since I was a child, I used to say that my country was the best one in the world. I love my territory, and I still think Colombia is an awesome place to live. However, that doesn´t mean that other countries are not. In fact, I am convinced that the strongest borders exist in our mind, which sometimes, unfortunately, prevent us from fully experiencing other cultures and customs. I remember now the smiling airport officer's words about the United States being an asylum, and I couldn't agree more. This is an asylum, where the daily craziness of each culture colliding teaches us how to coexist. Where those who dress up like medieval knights share with those like me, who can´t speak the language very well, and who no longer is afraid of making mistakes. I say, "What a wonderful experience, TGIF!"

24

Out of Hot Water: Culture Shock in the United States

Yuqing Wang, China

Flying to the US, I realized with a sigh that I had forgotten again what values each of these American coins in my hand stood for. Hardly had I taken another careful look at them when the airline attendant pushed a beverage carriage to my seat.

"Would you like something to drink?", she smiled politely.

"Hot water please," I replied without a second thought.

"Miss, you said…water, right?", she inquired very uncertainly.

"Yes, hot water please," I confirmed confidently.

A second later a glass of water filled with ice was handed to me. I was shocked to see a glass of cold water with ice cubes floating, which reminded me of Antarctica icebergs.

"Ma'am, may I have hot water?" I asked a small, controlled squeak.

"Oh," she replied after a minute's considered thought, "we don't have hot water here. We have hot tea and hot coffee."

For the first time, I found all of my years of learning English failed to cover an important aspect of the United States, that people would always put ice in their drinks, and that drinking hot water is never heard of. Back home in China, families would always boil a kettle of hot water for everybody to drink during the day. In schools, our drinking water faucet would always have one tab for hot water. It was unfathomable why Americans like to drink freezing iced drinks because ice will dilute the beverage, and iced drinks could cause irritation to those who have bad teeth that are sensitive to the cold. Yet even before I officially landed in the US, I had already learned a valuable piece of information about the new culture. So, there was a certain sense of achievement when I stepped out from the airplane into the warm, dazzling, sunlight-kissed terminal.

The memory of my first class at the University of Delaware still stays in a kind of fresh vivid daze— an unfamiliar mixture of restless excitement and anxiety. Looking around the big lecture room, the diversity of students is truly amazing. I would hardly see in a traditional Chinese classroom student from Jamaica, Mexico, Spain, France, India all at once, but here I can! No wonder America is coined, "a big melting pot" by Israel Zangwill.

Proud of its culture diversity, this "melting pot" offers a dynamic and lively academic atmosphere. In many classes, I am encouraged to think critically and to express my opinions freely in a heated discussion. Meanwhile, the professor serves not only as the source of knowledge, but also as a participant in a common search for understanding. Comparatively, it is much less common for my classmates and me to raise debates in the middle of a class in China, for fear of interrupting the instructor's thoughts. Rather, we are encouraged to note down the doubts and take them to meet the professor after the class, for one-on-one discussions. Here, creative thinking, heated discussions and critical debates are at the heart of many of my classes. "It is not just about examinations and regurgitating facts, it is about synthesizing knowledge and adopting it for life practices," one of my UD professors once remarked.

Equipped with classroom knowledge, I gained further practical experience through an internship with Winterthur Garden & Museum. From tour guiding to event coordinating, I learned extremely useful skills, such as personal communication, time management and task prioritization. This opportunity also introduced me to American fine arts, Delaware's history and DuPont family's heritage. At the end of the semester, I ran into a friend of mine whom I have not seen for a while.

"Oh Hey! How have you been?", she cheered happily, running over to give me a big hug.

"So nice to see you! I've been..." Thinking how to answer her in a simplest manner, I replied, "good, I have been good."

What I did not say was how rich the word "good" meant to me. Saturated in this word are the ups and downs, bitters and sweets, in this study abroad experience. Yet these challenges and adjustments are exactly what have tested me and molded me to become a more responsible, mature individual. Many international students, just like me and you, are those who acknowledged the language difficulties but never ceased to improve themselves; are those who experienced homesickness but never stopped to adapt to the new environment. We are willing to learn, ready for challenges and believe in "I can do this!"; We embrace differences and challenges and come out as a generation of strong, independent young adults. During this study abroad journey, I harvested priceless knowledge and mentalities, from understanding the culture of drinking iced water to critical thinking, self-discipline and open-mindedness— and they will continue to benefit me for the rest of my life and career.

25

My Story

Subramani Sockalingam, India

I hail from a small town in South India and my name is Subramani Sockalingam. Yes, it's a long and tough name for most people in the US and became an interesting challenge for others, and myself. So, I started going by Mani (supposed to be pronounced as "Money"), but people pronounce as Manny. It's definitely an ordeal, at least initially, to spell my name, if I call a help line for billing or customer service. However, when I started using the names of the US cities and states to spell my name, I found I could better communicate and even impressed the lady on the other side of the phone once.

I am good! First time in the US I was eating at a restaurant and the waiter asked, "Are you good?" I thought to myself what kind of a question is that? Of course, I am a good person. Then I realized they meant to ask if I wanted something or whether everything was alright. I am used to people asking, "do you need anything else?" or one of its variations which I am accustomed to from home. I am used to 'good' being the opposite of 'bad' and it is funny when people ask, "are you good?", and people say, "I am good". I started saying it too "I am good", and laugh inside every time I say it, thinking I have to boost myself.

When I say I am from India, some people inquire, "so you speak Indian?" Really there is no such language as Indian, as there are tens, if not hundreds, of different languages being spoken in India, with entirely different scripts. Living halfway around the world from home, friends in the US become the primary support system. I was fortunate enough to have a good support system in my friends around the US that helped me to get through some difficult times.

During my initial days in the US, I had some difficulty in understanding the accent of people and they had, and still have, difficulty in understanding my accent. I learned to consciously speak slowly and enunciate the words, to emulate an American accent, so people can better understand me. Since the British ruled India for a long time, I grew up with the British way of pronunciation and spelling. I worked to change my spellings, for example, "color" instead of "colour", "endeavor" and not "endeavour" and so on. The ability to speak the same language has been one tool that allowed me to better articulate and assimilate to a new culture.

In addition, the food in the US tasted bland relative to what I am used to growing up in India, which is the Mecca of spices, for which the British came to India. I learned to cook myself some Indian food, both for the spicy and economical aspects. My favorite being chicken curry, which I once cooked for a Christmas holiday party-people really enjoyed tasting it and wanted for the recipe! Nevertheless, living for a while in the US made me acclimatize to the less spicy food, and when I go home even my mom's cooking seems spicy. The ability to share my cultural heritage has allowed me to celebrate its depth without surrendering it for my new surroundings.

While language and food are vital elements of any culture, I have found volunteering to be another means to acclimate. I volunteered as a tutor for elementary school kids, and also on a crisis response team in Tempe, AZ. This provided me an opportunity to not only to make a positive difference but also to learn about the US local culture and customs, by interacting with people from all walks of life. Thus far, these experiences molded me into a person with broad mindedness, being non-judgmental, understanding, and empathizing with people, while embracing the opportunity to live in the present.

Overall, living in the US helped me learn so much- mostly about myself- and definitely cultivated a more mature individual in me. Specifically, it greatly improved my communication skills (both verbal and written) and the confident mindset with which I look at things. However, it's not without its challenges, especially the feeling of helplessness during difficult times back home. The Internet does help to stay connected with family and friends via video chatting. However, being so far away, one misses not only the local festivals but also happier family moments, like I recently became an uncle, as my sister became a mother. While I missed being there in person, I celebrated from a distance and embrace being able to transcend the time zones and distance with technology.

Being an international student is an enormous change, at least initially, to live in a different country, experience extremely different weather, different language and different culture. Stepping out of my shoes and talking to more people and engaging in different activities helped me to adjust to the new environment. More importantly, keeping an opening mind, "taking as it comes" and willing to learn attitude are, in my opinion, the mantra to survive and succeed.

26

The Dream of Living in a Different Country

Rodrigo Moreno, Chile

Ever since I was a teenager, I have dreamed of living in a foreign country. I am convinced that a study abroad experience is a time for learning not only the English language, but also learning about one's own self, personal growth and development. The experience of living in a foreign country has changed my life in many ways. This experience has been exciting because I have met many people from other countries. I have learned about their cultures and traditions and the most important thing is that some of them are my friends. Now, they are my family here. Also, I have had the opportunity to travel and visit places that I saw in magazines or Internet and I have enjoyed my amazing university life. My life changed in some ways such as I began to ride a bike for transportation. In my country, I only drove my car. This situation has been good for my health because I have lost weight. Nowadays, I am healthy and have a lot of energy. Then I surprised myself when I saw a lot of abandoned and rusty bikes. Some parked bikes had white or blue ties. Perhaps a good idea would be to donate them to other students.

Hello… is there anybody out there? When I first arrived in Newark on July 3rd, the city was empty, no one walked in the streets, just me. And I wanted to know where the inhabitants of the city were and what did they do during the day. Up to now, I don't have the answer. When I was walking through the city streets, it started to rain heavily, and I was not prepared for that kind of rain. I knew that it was summer, but in my country, summer is different, it is very dry and hot.

Then I understood that the weather in summer is warm, rainy and humid. I suffered a lot with the humidity. Actually, my first cultural shock was at the supermarket. I bought everything that I needed to start my student life in the apartment. I waited for a taxi for more than two hours, but it never came. Since I could not take a taxi, I had to return all the items I had bought. It was very embarrassing! Now I know that in Newark people don't take taxis because every person has a car. In my country, you can find a lot of taxis in every supermarket and everywhere. Every time that I remember that situation, it makes me laugh a lot.

In addition, I didn't understand when a cashier asked me if I had coupons. I watched carefully what other people bought. Days later, I understood that in magazines you could find discount coupons. Also, all Americans had a "magical key chain". It had a lot of little discount cards from different shops. Now, I can say that I have a beautiful one and I use it every day. Another situation that was really complicated was in the mall. On Sunday afternoon, I went to the mall. When I arrived there, a man on the loudspeaker said that the mall would be close in 30 minutes later, and I needed to buy some clothes. Then I realized that on Sundays some shops closed early.

On July 4th, I was completely immersed into the American culture because I celebrated the Independence Day. At the University, I read a poster. It was an invitation to celebrate the Independence Day. I went with some friends and we enjoyed a delicious picnic and went to watch spectacular fireworks at a beautiful place near a lake. People were very friendly and kind. On the contrary, in my country we celebrate our Independence Day on September 18th and it is very different. People eat and drink so much and dance our National Dance called Cueca.

On the other hand, I miss two things about my country. My family: I miss my family life in Chile, celebrating holidays and my relatives' birthdays. The other thing is the food, especially avocado and bread. In the city avocado is really expensive, so I have bought it only once. There is no bread like in my country. I have found a few kinds of bread. But I enjoy American food, such as baby ribs, cheeseburgers and chicken wings. They are delicious!!!

Finally, I can say that this time has been the best of all my life.

27

A New Culture: Help Me, I'm Drowning!

Karim Rebiai, Belgium

Beyond the obvious educational and career-broadening aspects, I find that living and studying abroad is an intrinsically transformative experience. The intellectual challenge of life outside of the "cultural cocoon" – that is, outside of the home environment – can be socially and inwardly alienating. On the one hand, the cultural demands of life in a different country, the "outside" world, entails the learning of a completely different language, the "reworking" of your own habits, and a dire desire to fit in. On the other hand, the intellectual aspect of the journey, the "inside" world, is characterized by frustration born out of naturally hindered communication. This overwhelming frustration leads to a natural self-refashioning and to the slow solitary confinement of our personality. However, after the necessary period of adjustment and the achievement of inner balance, the true adventure begins; we grow smarter, more open, more confident and, in many cases, wiser.

The outside world that we have to explore is one of different habits, and the surrounding culture in which we land can be so unsettling that we feel lost and somewhat out of place at the beginning of our "odyssey". As a Belgian, I am personally accustomed to kissing acquaintances on the cheek as a form of greeting or leave-taking, whereas in the United States, it is seen as an invasion of privacy. Our natural European (dare I say of French origin?) proclivity for physical contact as a form of greeting is regarded as some sort of idiosyncratic behavior that breaches the boundaries of Americans' personal comfort zone. After a few uncomfortable situations, I learned to keep my distance. This "distance" seemed to contradict with the American habit of literally flashing a broad grin at complete strangers when making eye contact. Habits such as these are part of a larger and more complex social code of conduct to which we need to grow accustomed, all the while facing the more laborious challenge: the communicative one. Indeed, the prime objective of an experience abroad is to learn a foreign language and to have a full immersion experience in the target culture. I quickly realized how different the communicative challenges of being a UD student were from those I faced in my English classes in Belgium. Throughout our linguistic education, we are trying not to drown in this ocean of cultural twists and turns, but to stay afloat and, if feasible, to "swim" or to "fit into" a new culture.

Nonetheless, "fitting in" is a much more convoluted task than merely understanding a new culture and slowly learning a new language. Indeed, while educating ourselves in the ways of the host community, we literally have to change on the inside and compromise. One of the greatest challenges of this experience is undeniably to try to cope with a limited knowledge of the target language. Lacking the linguistic skills to express our own thought patterns is an incredibly frustrating and demoralizing feeling that many of us experience. With a personality constrained by the language barrier, international students have to settle for expressing basic ideas and adopt a somewhat shallow discourse. These linguistic constraints lead to the emergence of some sort of "new personality" and thus to a "self-refashioning" brought about by a craving to communicate in the foreign language. Moreover, speaking a different language is an extremely strenuous task, a genuine intellectual workout. Using only the foreign language all day long is exhausting. As a graduate student who also serves as a Teaching Assistant, I find myself completely "wiped out" on Tuesday nights after having taught three classes and attended my three-hour literature seminar. The combined outcome of the two aforementioned factors, the self-refashioning of the personality and the wearying aspect of communicating in a different language, may lead to a solitary confinement of our personality. We feel trapped inside of our own mind with a "self" that we cannot share and, even if we try, it is utterly exhausting. This state of mind, this deep and undisclosed desire to be understood, is called "homesickness". Drawn into the new culture, unable to be ourselves and tired of trying, we feel nostalgic for "home", a familiar place where everything is easier and more instinctive.

Fortunately, this difficult period is not the apex of the journey; quite the contrary! After the rapturous feeling of starting a new adventure and the ineluctable, and the yet short-lived despondency following the realization of cultural and linguistic constraints – i.e., homesickness –, we are ready to fashion a better version of ourselves. Enriched by our adaptability and our newly gained confidence, most of our apprehensions slowly melt away, leaving our mind open to the vastness of the world we live in. Indeed, instead of missing our old habits, we learn about new ones that complete our "self" and we "grow up" culturally. Moreover, we transcend our need to unilaterally learn from others and actually start sharing our home culture with them, helping our hosts see their culture in a new light. In this spirit of cultural exchange, the learning of a foreign language becomes considerably more effective, and as we expand our linguistic knowledge, our latent (native) personality slowly reemerges and fuses with the new mature version of ourselves: we have become a citizen of the world.

To decide to live abroad and to acculturate to a new environment is to accept to embark on a life-changing journey, requiring patience, motivation and discipline. On the outside, we might think we are out of our depth, swimming in a new and frightening culture, startled by unfamiliar social customs. On the inside, we have to suffer pro tempore from "linguistic schizophrenia" and tortuously remodel our social self, turning the original "us" into a hermit. However, these phases are only the first steps of the journey. The next step is one of cultural, linguistic, and personal enrichment: we adapt, grow up, and become stronger. Having achieved equilibrium in a new culture, nobody wants the journey to end and to go back to their previous life, quite the contrary. Now open to the world, we are looking for the next adventure, longing for the next revolutionary experience. What are you waiting for? Dive in!

Appendix

List of Contributors

Name	Country	Level	Major	Year of Essay
Sarah Yacoba Coomson	Ghana	Graduate	Biological Sciences	2020
Abhinav Prabhakar	India	Graduate	Chemistry & Biochemistry	2020
Emma Perichon	France	Undergraduate	Communication	2020
Jady Young Perez	Panama	Undergraduate	Environmental Engineering	2020
Norha Almousa	Saudi Arabia	English Language	English Language	2020
Essa Nahari	Saudi Arabia	English Language	English Language	2020
Carolina Gomez	Colombia	Undergraduate	Biomedical Engineering	2018
Josefina Fernandez-Davila	Peru	Undergraduate	International Business Studies	2018
Fabian Martin Rempfer	Germany	Graduate	English	2018
Ashwini Sansare	India	Graduate	Biomechanics & Movement Science	2018
Aishah Moafa	Saudi Arabia	English Language	English Language Institute	2018
Somi Kim	South Korea	English Language	English Language Institute	2018
John Wambui	Kenya	Graduate	Urban Affairs & Public Policy	2017
Mehmet Altingoz	Turkey	Graduate	Water Science & Policy	2017
Edgar Salazar	Colombia	Graduate	Electrical & Computer Engineering	2017
Chamath Chandrasekera	Sri Lanka	Graduate	Biological Sciences	2016
Xueyao Liang	China	Undergraduate	History	2016
Ugochukwu Nsofor	Nigeria	Graduate	Electrical & Computer Engineering	2016
Kervin Zamora	Honduras	Graduate	Public Administration	2015
Ashish Chouhan	India	Graduate	Mechanical Engineering	2015
Hanna Olsson	Sweden	Undergraduate	Hotel & Restaurant Management	2015
Olga Parshina	Russia	Graduate	Linguistics & Cognitive Science	2014
Byron Acosta	Colombia	English Language	English Language Institute	2014
Yuqing Wang	China	Graduate	Liberal Studies	2014
Subramani Sockalingam	India	Graduate	Mechanical Engineering	2013
Rodrigo Moreno	Chile	English Language	English Language Institute	2013
Karim Rebiai	Belgium	Graduate	Foreign Languages & Pedagogy	2013

Related Titles

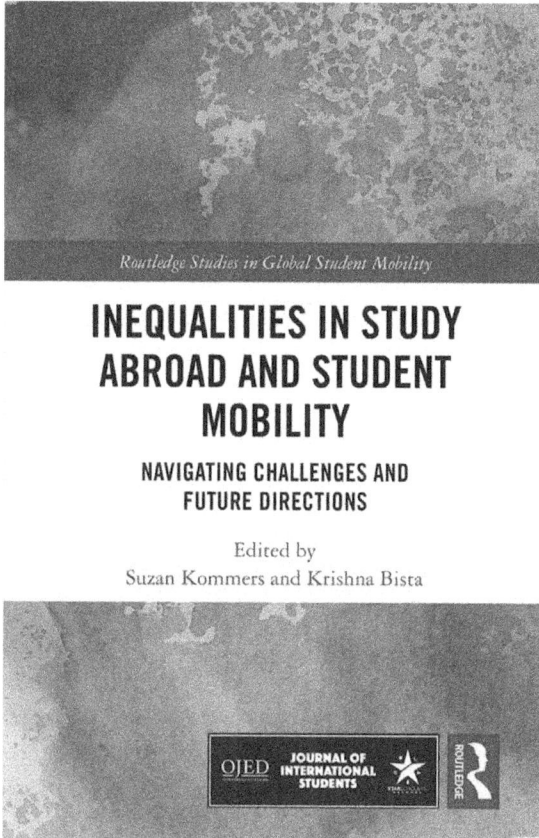

Routledge Studies in Global Student Mobility

INEQUALITIES IN STUDY ABROAD AND STUDENT MOBILITY

NAVIGATING CHALLENGES AND FUTURE DIRECTIONS

Edited by
Suzan Kommers and Krishna Bista

"This book serves as an important resource for international educators and practitioners at a critical time when institutions are grappling with inequality issues in Study Abroad and student mobility. It offers both practical and research-driven insights that can guide institutional policy and practice in promoting diversity, empathy, and inclusive internationalization on campus."

Ravi Ammigan, *Associate Deputy Provost, University of Delaware, USA*

"Inequalities in Study Abroad and Student Mobility sheds light on a critically important issue that has been far too often ignored, namely, social inequality in study abroad. Utilizing a comparative cross-national approach, this edited volume offers a highly welcomed examination of a gnawing concern for all of us engaged in international education."

William I. Brustein, *Vice President, West Virginia University, USA*

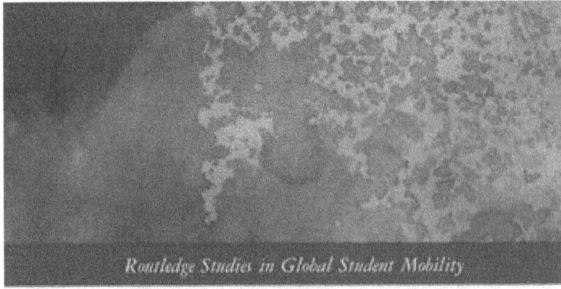

INTERNATIONAL STUDENTS AT US COMMUNITY COLLEGES

OPPORTUNITIES, CHALLENGES, AND SUCCESSES

Edited by
Gregory F. Malveaux and Krishna Bista

Foreword by Linda Serra Hagedorn

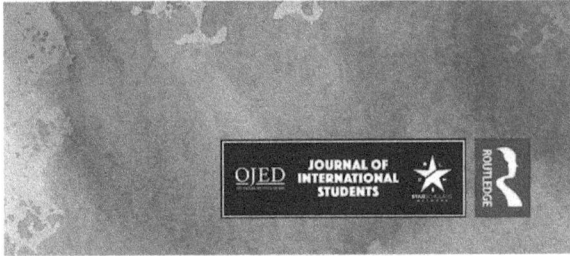

America's community colleges have become attractive options for international students for several reasons. They are the largest single segment of American higher education; they enroll a diverse student body; they are affordable; they provide curricula that are focused on skill building; and they offer a pathway to a baccalaureate or higher degree. International students also contribute significantly to the community colleges they attend, both financially and through their interactions with American students. The knowledgeable authors of International Students at US Community Colleges: Opportunities, Challenges, and Successes provide a valuable resource for college leaders who are interested in internationalizing their campuses and serving their international students.

George R. Boggs, Ph.D., *Superintendent/ President Emeritus, Palomar College, President and CEO Emeritus, American Association of Community Colleges, USA*

From their inception, community colleges have played a critical role in furthering our nation's historic mission of educating for democracy. This book offers invaluable insights into how faculty and administrators can fulfill a 21st-century equity mandate by ensuring community colleges are places of welcome and belonging for international students, while positioning this growing student population for success in a global knowledge economy.

Lynn Pasquerella, PhD, *President, Association of American Colleges and Universities, USA*

Routledge Studies in Global Student Mobility

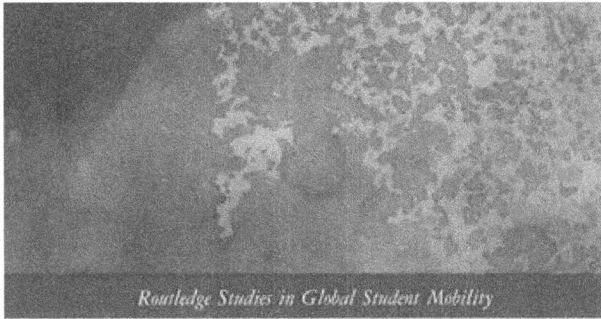

CRITICAL PERSPECTIVES ON EQUITY AND SOCIAL MOBILITY IN STUDY ABROAD

INTERROGATING ISSUES OF UNEQUAL ACCESS AND OUTCOMES

Edited by
Chris Glass and Peggy Gesing

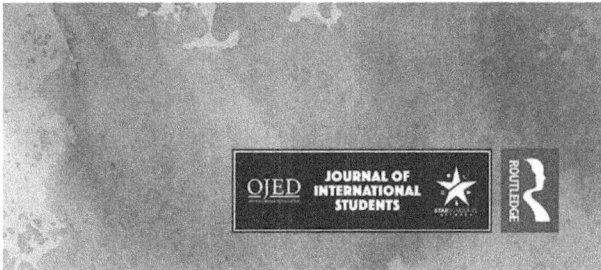

Without reservation, I applaud this multi-faceted and in-depth examination laying bare the stratification and inequities of study abroad. This book challenges the vestiges of privilege and provides ways that equity can be infused within study abroad.

Linda Serra Hagedorn, *Professor Emeritus, Iowa State University, USA*

This volume addresses important aspects of both access and outcome of global student mobility, by a diverse team of scholars from a rich variety of perspectives.

Yenbo Wu, *Associate Vice President, Division of International Education,*
San Francisco State University, USA

This is a must read for all involved with developing, managing and accessing study abroad programming.

Brian Whalen, *Executive Director, American International Recruitment Council*
International Education Leadership Fellow, University at Albany, USA